ELEPHANTS IN PARIS

A memoir

Scott Corey

BookLocker
Trenton, Georgia

Paperback ISBN: 978-1-958878-06-4
Hardcover ISBN: 978-1-958878-07-1
Ebook ISBN: 979-8-88531-371-1

Published by BookLocker.com, Inc., Trenton, Georgia.

Printed on acid-free paper.

BookLocker.com, Inc.
2023

First Edition

Library of Congress Cataloguing in Publication Data
Corey, Scott
Elephants in Paris by Scott Corey
Library of Congress Control Number: 2022920314

Back cover painting by George Corey.

ALSO BY SCOTT COREY

Whistling for Hippos – a memoir of life in West Africa

What we have once enjoyed we can never lose. All that we love deeply becomes a part of us.

Helen Keller

CONTENTS

Author's Note

The names of many individuals in this book have been changed to protect their privacy. I have also omitted the name of the elephant.

Preface: Elephants in Paris

I anticipated many things happening to me in Paris. I expected to see picturesque views of the Seine, to sit with friends at charming cafes for hours, to tour historic sites and quarters made famous by artists and writers. I expected to see sleek young women strolling along the rue de Rivoli and around the Opera. I thought perhaps I would be introduced to a few celebrities or writers who were just getting established. But I never expected to round a corner from my apartment on the rue de Malte and bump head-long into an elephant.

As the reader will learn later in this book, my wife and I lived in an apartment at 17 rue de Malte near the Place de la Republique. This was a quaint corner opposite the Métro Oberkampf with a wonderful patisserie, decent cafes, and a wine shop nearby. Our apartment was on the third floor above a butcher shop that sold rotisserie chickens. The delicious scent of these roasting fowl wafted up and into our open windows throughout the day.

Around the corner was the rue Crussol, a narrow street that led to the Boulevard du Temple and the *Cirque d'Hiver* or Winter Circus. This amphitheater was home to a small cast of circus performers and a few animals. In Hemingway's day it also was used for indoor bicycle racing. The main entrance to the *Cirque d'Hiver* was on the rue Amelot, but the loading entrance was on the rue Crussol.

On the morning of my encounter with the elephant, I was in a rush to catch the number 35 bus to school. As I hadn't had time to eat lunch, I thought I would grab a spring roll from an Asian shop halfway down the street.

Hurrying from our apartment building, I was rounding the corner past the rotisserie and butcher shop and up the rue Crussol when …

WHAM.

I collided head-long with an elephant.

An ELEPHANT!

On a sidewalk in Paris.

The animal was being directed through the loading entrance of the circus when it broke free of its handler and came trotting down the street. I imagined it was tired of being cooped up indoors and wanted to stroll around Paris like everyone else and to breathe in the fresh air.

I glanced up just in time to see a massive grey head and trunk looming over me. It seemed the elephant was as surprised as I was at the collision. I didn't feel any danger. I could imagine him saying, "*Excusez-moi*," and then shuffling off to one side to let me pass.

Behind him, the handler was running down the street, shouting wildly and waving a long wooden elephant prod with a brass hook at the end. I later learned this instrument was called an Ankush.

To me, the situation was hilarious. The last thing I expected to bump into on a Paris sidewalk was a promenading elephant. But as I thought about it later, the encounter seemed to reflect my existence in Paris. Because when you live there, you never know what to expect. The most outrageous things can happen in the City of Light–from viewing beautifully manicured gardens to impoverished quarters lined with trash and streaked with urine; from comic encounters with bizarre bohemians, to the blood-flow of terrorist attacks. You never know when the next person you meet will offer you a glass of wine or try to pick your pocket.

These extremes add to the heightened sensitivity of the city, to its energy, and the possibility that anything can happen and often does–including bumping into an elephant when you're strolling to lunch.

Chapter 1
Boy in the Fringed Cowboy Jacket

O'Hare International Airport
September, 1981

Our journey to Paris started with a French boy in a fringed cowboy jacket. He was slowly making his way down the aisle of the Icelandic Airlines flight to Luxembourg City. I knew he would sit in our row. I knew this because I had noticed him in the boarding area and Murphy's Law Number One of Air Travel states that if you notice someone in the gate area, they will inevitably sit near you. At least, it had always proven true for me.

Murphy's Law Number Two states that if there is a young mother with a crying child at the gate, they will *not* be in your row—they will sit directly behind you. The child will scream bloody murder the entire flight, and if they are old enough, they will also systematically kick your seat like a conga drum. I hadn't noticed any mothers with babies at the gate, so I relaxed into my seat and prayed for a tranquil flight. I had, however, seen the boy in the fringed jacket and watched with a mixture of curiosity and fatigue as he edged down the aisle.

When he reached our row, he glanced at his boarding pass, up at the row number, and then at me. He had dark curly hair and an eager, engaging grin. I glanced down at his feet to see if he was wearing cowboy boots. He wasn't. Below the edge of his faded jeans was a pair of high-top black Converse tennis shoes.

"*C'est moi,*" he said, pointing to the open seat beside my wife.

I began to stand up and let him through when he held up his right index finger and grinned again.

"Ah, hah," he said and scooted through the empty row in front of us and around to the other side. A red, white, and blue Air France bag

1

hung from his shoulder. He put this in an overhead compartment and settled into the seat beside us.

My wife smiled at him. She had the genetic gift of liking everyone. I was more withdrawn socially and–especially on airplanes–preferred to sit quietly and read, listen to an audio book, or sleep.

Within a few moments, they were chatting amiably and after a few more minutes, Claudia leaned over to me and whispered, "His name is Lucien. He's fifteen and has been visiting friends in Colorado. This was his first trip to the states. His family lives in Paris."

"Wow," I said and closed my eyes.

We were also on our way to Paris. For the past two years, Claudia and I had lived in West Africa. As we were preparing to leave the bush lands, an acquaintance had taken a letter from his pocket and waved it under my nose.

"From a school in Paris," he said. "They're looking for teachers who can speak French and have overseas experience. You should apply. You'd be perfect."

I wrote to the school and requested a job interview. A month later we stood shivering on the Place l'Odeon. It was July and sunny in Paris, but during the dry season in the bushland, the temperature often rose to 120 degrees. This made the French weather feel chilly. I did not expect this and hadn't brought a jacket. So, to keep warm, I wore two shirts and a sweater.

The English Language School had offered me the job and now, in September, we were returning to Paris to live.

Our flight from O'Hare was about to take off. I can't count the amount of times I've fallen asleep before take-off and awakened later at thirty thousand feet. There is something lulling about the steady hum of the engines, combined with the cramped boredom of the narrow seats, that knocks me out. Ironically, once the airplane is in the air, I can't go back to sleep no matter how hard I try.

Eventually, we touched down in Luxembourg and made our way through the beautiful city to the train station. The final leg of our trip to Paris was made in an *entraîneur de deuxième classe*–or Second-Class coach. Lucien accompanied us. By now Claudia had essentially adopted him and I was computing how much it would cost us to put him through college. Of course, only the best university would do for a boy of his character and intelligence.

As Claudia taught Lucien to play gin rummy on the train, I unfolded a map of Paris. Our train was scheduled to arrive in the Gare du Nord at 9pm. In the haste to catch our flight–which included a frantic return to my in-laws' house to retrieve passports left on a bedroom dresser–I hadn't made any hotel reservations.

This is where serendipity entered our lives–if you don't count Lucien being seated beside us, which was undoubtedly the first step in this bit of good fortune.

"Lucien's parents are going to meet him at the station," Claudia informed me. "He says they can find us a hotel."

"Wow," I said. "I don't know how you do it."

"Maybe if you'd played a few games of cards with him," she said.

Nicolas and Lena Allard greeted us on the platform as we stepped off the train. He was tall with long gray hair combed back over his collar and she was small and lean with blonde hair and sharp features. We waited self-consciously as Lucien explained our situation. His parents nodded as he talked and then gazed at us.

"Thank you for keeping an eye on him," his mother said. "You know how it is when teenagers travel alone. We are always a bit worried."

"Of course," we both agreed.

"You are looking for a hotel?" Nicolas asked.

"Yes," I replied. "We didn't have time to make a reservation."

He nodded. "I know one on the rue de Sampaix. Not far. We will take you."

Grabbing our bags, we followed the Allards through the scuffed lobby of the Gare du Nord and out to the rue de Dunkerque with its traffic and yellow arc lights.

As we strolled, I breathed in the night air and the scent of Paris. I loved the city with its tall apartment buildings, streets designed by George-Eugène Haussmann, sidewalk cafes, the Seine twinkling in the lights of passing boats, the bridges–especially the Pont Neuf and the Pont Alexandre III–and of course, the Latin Quarter. Every time I arrived in Paris, a surge of excitement ran through me.

"What is your occupation?" Nicolas asked as we turned onto the rue du Faubourg Saint Denis.

"I'm a teacher," I replied.

"*Ah bon,*" he said. "*Mathématiques?*"

"English."

"Of course."

"And you?" I asked.

"*Journaliste,*" he replied.

The hotel was a narrow, four-story building painted gray with a large glass window and a door leading into the lobby. A blue neon sign blinked the simple announcement of HOTEL above our heads.

"*Ça va?*" Nicolas asked.

"Perfect," I said.

Lena spoke up. "Are you free for dinner on Wednesday?"

I turned to Claudia.

"Do we have plans?" I asked.

"Let me think," she said with a smirk.

We had no plans for Wednesday evening or any other evening.

"I guess not," she replied.

"*Bon,*" Lena said.

She jotted their address on a scrap of paper and handed it to Claudia. A bond had already developed between them and it was obvious that from now on, the women would organize all social interactions. Nicolas and I were simply along for the ride. We shook hands, kissed cheeks, and waved as the Allards headed toward the Métro. Then we opened the glass door and stepped into the hotel lobby.

A woman behind the counter gazed at us with total indifference. She wore a dirty smock pulled over a tattered sweater. Her fingernails were stained brown from cigarettes. The burning tip of one jutted from between her fingers. I immediately had misgivings. I got the feeling that if I dropped dead in the lobby, she would only lean over the counter, gaze at me, and mutter, "*Ah boff.*"

Nicolas Allard had suggested this place, so it must be okay. Madame Apathy-as I now thought of her-asked for our passports, jotted down our information, and gave us a room key. I had been prepared to spend the evening in an exhausting search to find a hotel room and now *voila*-thanks to the Allards, we had one within a few minutes.

The third-floor room was tiny, with a sagging double bed and red wallpaper. I imagined it was rented by the hour in the daytime. But we were weary after our transatlantic flight and only wanted to sleep. I changed my mind, however, when I tossed my bag onto the bed and it moved; not the bed itself, but something on the bed. The room was crawling with cockroaches.

"Oh my God!" Claudia exclaimed.

"Don't set anything down," I warned, grabbing my bag.

We leaped out of the room and slammed the door.

Claudia gave a shudder. "I haven't seen anything like that since Ouagadougou," she cried, referring to a town we had visited in the sub-Sahara.

I gazed at the door and thought I saw a slight rumbling movement, as if thousands of roaches were on the other side pressing against the wood. It was probably my imagination, but still ...

"We can't stay here," Claudia said.

"No shit," I replied.

We hurried down the stairs and back to the counter. Madame Apathy looked even more detached when we told her about the insects.

"If you wish to wait," she offered, "I will have the room fumigated."

We had been through this before at a hotel in Abidjan and the insecticide fumes emanating from the mattress during the night had nearly killed us. We awakened the next morning looking pale, shaking, and with severe headaches. Not again. There was no way this was going to end well when it was nearly ten o'clock at night.

"We're leaving," I said and tossed the room key onto the counter.

Madame Apathy shrugged and tore up our passport information.

"Gees," I gasped as we slammed through the entrance and out to the street.

Claudia's body gave a final spasm of revulsion.

"Can you imagine trying to sleep in there?" she asked.

I laughed. The room was so gross it was amusing. "No way."

She laughed too. "Where to now?"

I glanced up the street and saw two other hotel signs. "Let's try those."

Picking up our bags and giving them a violent shake to see if any cockroaches dropped off, we headed up the street. Unfortunately, both hotels had signs blinking in their windows that said *Complet* – which meant no vacancy.

"Feel like a stroll?" I asked.

"You're joking, right?" Claudia responded.

A corner café had outside tables and since this was early September, the evening weather was pleasant.

"I could use a beer," I said.

Claudia gave a sigh. "Okay."

She ordered a Kier and I ordered a Pelforth Brune—a full-bodied dark beer. It felt good to relax for a few minutes and to appreciate being in Paris once again, even though we had no place to sleep.

I was just finishing my beer and thinking about ordering another when I spied the glow of a brightly lit sign around the corner. Could it possibly be another hotel?

"Look," I said, pointing.

We paid our check and left the cafe.

As we rounded the corner, a neon sign announced the *Deux Hemispheres Hotel*.

The front of the hotel was painted white, with large wood-framed windows and a cheerful front entrance. Black wrought-iron gratings decorated the second-floor windows. The hotel seemed pleasant and I was optimistic.

A slender man with dark hair and a thick moustache greeted us as we entered. A tag on his maroon vest informed us this was Salim.

"We would like a room for the night," I said.

Salim clapped his hands together cheerfully. "Yes, yes," he said. "No Problem."

We went through the check-in procedure again and received another room key.

"We are all Algerians here," Salim announced with a broad smile. "The counter staff, the femme de ménage ... everyone."

"That's nice," Claudia said.

Our room was on the second floor. We entered with some trepidation, expecting at any moment to see a tide of cockroaches advancing on us from the darkened corners. But the room was clean and well-maintained. This time I didn't mind tossing my bag onto the bedspread.

Claudia hesitated in the doorway, her eyes scanning every surface and wall.

"I guess it's okay," she said at last.

Just to make sure, I pulled back the bedcovers to reveal a starched white sheet.

"Clear here," I said.

"Thank God," she murmured. "I can't keep my eyes open any longer."

"It was the Kier," I said.

"Maybe," she said and stepped into the bathroom.

That night I lay with my arms behind my head and listened to traffic passing on the Boulevard de Magenta. Hotels and apartment buildings in Paris had a particular scent. I imagined it came from the type of cleaning products used. Every time I breathed in that scent, it reminded me of the famous artists and writers who had lived here, of the books about Paris I'd read, the museums I'd visited, the paintings I'd seen, and my heart beat a little faster. Finally, after so many years of dreaming about it, I was going to live in Paris. I was going to get up every morning, open the shutters, breathe in Paris, and feel the hum of the city around me.

Chapter 2
The Feckin' American

It amazes me when I consider how often we exhaust ourselves in planning our futures-like African weaver birds constructing elaborate nests-and then a chance encounter, communication, or conversation changes everything. I had never considered living in Paris. My dream was to live in London. I loved British rock & roll and several of my favorite authors were British. My parents were both stationed there in the military and told me stories about how much they enjoyed the country and the people.

After my freshmen year of college, I arranged through an international exchange program to work in London for the summer. I was to work at the Swiss Fair restaurant in Leicester Square. Had I ever worked at a restaurant before? No. But if it gave me the chance to live in England, I would learn.

Upon my arrival, I checked into the Regent's Park Hotel in Gloucester Place. It was a pleasant hotel, and I was soon out seeing Number 10 Downing Street, Piccadilly Circus, Trafalgar Square, Camden Market, and other famous sites. I ate fish and chips and drank Newcastle brown ale and bought an umbrella when it began to rain. (Incidentally, Murphy's Law Number Three states that if you buy an umbrella on vacation because it is raining, it will never rain another day of your trip and you'll be carrying the damned thing around forever.)

I was a very green nineteen-year-old at the time and proud of the moustache I'd grown that spring–one I believed made me look like the actor Tom Selleck. At least, in my imagination.

That evening I was eating dinner alone in the Regent's Park dining room when a gentleman in a dark suit asked if he might sit at my table. The dining room was crowded, so I said of course. This was normal etiquette in Europe.

Dinner was served, and we began talking about politics. Mr. Denham was a distinguished-looking man with thinning silver hair.

"You know why we're having so many problems politically," he said, sipping at his after-dinner cognac.

"The economy?" I offered.

He dismissed my response with the shake of a manicured fingernail and a dry chuckle.

"Many people think that," he said. "But the truth is … it's a conspiracy."

"A conspiracy?" I asked.

Mr. Denham's eyes flitted suspiciously around the crowded room. He lit a filter cigarette and leaned toward me. I could smell cognac on his breath.

"The Jews," he whispered sternly. "They control everything."

I looked at the man more closely now. He was about sixty-five with finely wrinkled skin, dark eyebrows above pale, unflinching eyes, and an arrogant jaw. From his appearance, he looked as if he might be in business or politics.

A Jewish conspiracy?

I suddenly pictured Mr. Denham in a German officer's uniform— perhaps SS. I wondered if Denham was his real name. Probably something more like Deisler, Delbruck, or *Dummkopf.*

He must have taken my bewilderment as acceptance, because he ordered another cognac and went on at length.

I watched him suspiciously now, wondering why he was talking to me, wondering about his motives. He had a slight accent to his English, but I couldn't determine the origin

The previously crowded dining room was half empty now.

"It's all very complicated, but true," he said, nodding thoughtfully.

I pushed back my chair. "Well," I said. "I have to be going."

Mr. Denham gazed at me appraisingly. "If you'd like to continue our conversation," he offered. "I have a bottle of brandy in my room."

"Thanks," I said. "But I have a few calls to make."

I walked out to Gloucester Place. The rain had stopped (because I'd purchased the umbrella). I walked around for a while, trying to adjust to the seven-hour time difference, and finally stepped into an Irish pub. Sitting on a heavy wooden bar stool, I watched the patrons at the surrounding tables. A young woman with curly red hair was laughing delightedly at one table. A group of young people-probably students–gathered around her.

As a pint of Murphy's Irish Stout appeared in front of me, I thought of the stories my parents had told me about London. I was finally here. And tomorrow morning I would go to Leicester Square and find out about my job. I forgot about the strange man in the dark suit with his anti-Semitic theories and instead listened to the invigorating Irish pub music. After a while, a scruffy young man in a tattered army jacket came around the tables with an old coffee can that had a slit in the top. He was collecting for Sinn Féin–the political branch of the Irish Republican Army.

The manager of the Swiss Fair restaurant was slender, with blonde hair slicked back and a professional air of aloofness. Herr Ulrich glanced over my papers thoughtfully and reached for a pen.

"You have your work permit," he said, signing his name to a form. "So, you will begin tomorrow morning at ten o'clock. Okay?"

"Fine," I said. "And my days off?"

"Sunday."

"Sunday? I work six days a week?"

He looked surprised. "Naturally. Anything less is considered part-time."

Well, I told myself, if I got off work early enough, I would still have time to see London. I was looking forward to visiting Soho.

"Also," Herr Ulrich continued. "You will have to shave off that moustache."

"Europeans wear moustaches," I protested.

Herr Ulrich nodded. "Yes, but they do not look like yours. In Europe men wear thin moustaches like, um, Errol Flynn or David Niven. Not like a cowboy."

"I see."

"So," he said, walking to the door of his office. "If you want to work at the Swiss Fair, you must shave.

Employees of the Swiss Fair lived in a boarding house in Earl's Court. Rent for a room was deducted from our wages. It was a brief ride from Leicester Square on the Underground. I took the paper Herr Ulrich had given me and rode out to Earl's Court. It was a lifeless neighborhood of row houses and boarding houses. I contacted the landlady, who directed me to a street-front room on the second floor. Each floor looked the same, with a long corridor and a narrow staircase at the end. There were six floors.

"If you want to take a bath," the landlady told me. "It's on the top floor."

I reported to work promptly at ten o'clock the next morning and was given a starched white shirt and apron. Herr Ulrich's assistant manager showed me around the restaurant. He introduced me to the other staff, most of them German, Swiss, or Irish. I worked hard all day-busing tables, carrying food, and rolling napkins. At six o'clock, I glanced at my watch, expecting my shift to be over. No one said anything.

"It's six o'clock," I mentioned to another waiter.

He looked at the clock in the kitchen as we carried in a tray of dirty plates. The kitchen was steaming hot and smelled of grease.

"That's right," he said in his Swiss accent.

"Don't we get off?"

He looked at me. "The dinner crowd will be coming soon. There's no time to let up now."

"But ..." I began hopelessly. I wanted to see Portobello Road. I wanted to eat Indian food, and wander through Piccadilly Circus. I didn't want to be stuck here with my splotched white apron, tired feet, and a tray of dirty dishes.

"We usually get off at eleven," he added.

"Eleven?" Five more hours! I could hardly believe it. Giving the plates to the dishwasher, I rubbed my aching back and groaned.

That night I felt as if the kitchen staff had beaten me with a cricket bat and sprayed me with cooking oil. As I rode to Earl's Court on the Underground, I almost fell asleep. I thought about tumbling into bed with my clothes on, but the image was too gross. I couldn't sleep covered in grease.

The stairs looked like something out of an M. C. Escher drawing, winding this way and back in a confusing series of landings and corridors.

I found the bathroom vacant at the top of the stairs, filled the tub with hot water, and sank in. The warm water relaxed me so that I could hardly keep my eyes open, let alone walk back down all those stairs to my room. I gazed at my greasy restaurant clothes draped across the chair and then at my towel. It was midnight. Why get dressed again when I was only going downstairs to my room?

The towel wasn't very large, but it touched around my waist and provided enough covering for a quick dash. Gathering up my clothes and shoes, I opened the bathroom door and peeked down the corridor. I listened for a moment and didn't hear anyone coming. Tip-toeing out to the landing, I clutched the towel in one hand and bolted, taking the stairs two at a time. When I reached my door, I jumped inside and slammed it quickly behind me. Safe!

A squeal of surprise erupted from the room. Turning, I saw six German girls from the restaurant staring at me. Snacks and magazines lay across the beds. I was in the wrong room.

Damn!

After a moment of shock, the girls recognized me and exploded into laughter. One of them pointed to my skimpy towel and bounced on the bed. I didn't speak German, but I blurted my apologies and jumped into the hallway.

Now I was in trouble, because I didn't know which floor I was on. Coming down the stairs, I had been certain I was on the second floor. Obviously, I had miscounted. Every floor looked the same.

It was after midnight. What to do?

As I was standing there bewildered with the towel clutched around me – a towel that seemed much smaller now than when I darted from the bathroom-the door cracked open and one of the German girls peeked out.

I smiled at her, embarrassed.

"You are lost?" she asked.

"Yes," I said, blushing.

She had pale blonde hair and sparkling blue eyes. I had noticed her at the restaurant and thought about asking her out to a pub. Now she would think I was a fool.

"On what floor are you staying?" she persisted.

"The second."

She glanced at my towel. "You must go down one more. This is the third."

I thanked her and started for the stairs. As she closed the door behind me, she muttered something in German and the other girls laughed again. If I had a comedic personality, I might have dropped the towel when I entered the girls' room and turned my overwhelming embarrassment into a prank. But that wasn't me-unfortunately.

I worked at the Swiss Fair until the end of the week, but it was apparent the job and I didn't match. For starters, I had not yet shaved off my moustache. Every morning the assistant manager pulled me aside and told me to do it. Each morning I hesitated. By Thursday, he was adamant.

"If the moustache is not gone by tomorrow," he snapped. "Do not come to work."

Outside the Underground at Earl's Court, a man was selling bags of Bing cherries. I bought a bag and ate them as I walked around the neighborhood, trying to decide what to do. I had planned to work at the Swiss Fair for most of the summer. Quitting meant I would have to cut short my trip. If I left London, where would I go?

The answer came to me as I finished the last cherry.

Liverpool!

In school, my best friend was a boy named Dennis Callahan. He was from Liverpool and looked a bit like George Harrison. He played this up to attract girls. I had often spent time at his house and had gotten to know his 'mum' and his three sisters. Recently, they had moved back to Liverpool without Dennis. I was sure Mrs. Callahan wouldn't mind if I dropped in for a day or two. I phoned her from one of the quaint red telephone booths and she said they would be glad to see me.

The following morning, I resigned as tactfully as I could from the restaurant (the assistant manager expected it when I entered still looking like a cowboy) and then went directly to Victoria Station. As I passed a record shop, a clerk was putting a Paul McCartney album in the window. I took this as a good omen.

The train to Liverpool was crowded and I found my way into a compartment and took a seat. For a week I had been searching for the real English, not just foreigners or various members of the Empire, but the people I had read so much about and of whom my parents had spoken so wistfully. Now, by chance, I had stumbled into a compartment full of classic English types. The refined woman who sat across from me bore a striking resemblance to Julie Andrews. Beside her sat a soldier with sandy-blonde hair and a clipped moustache who explained that he was on leave from India. Next to me was a parson. Somehow, I had inadvertently bumped into the cast of Clue. Though somewhat discouraged that I was an American, they were all pleased to hear my family had come from Edinburgh, Scotland.

"Though we don't pronounce it Edinburgh," Miss Andrews explained with a roll of her tongue. "We say *Edinborough.*"

"Before you spoke, I thought you might be from an Indian Regiment with that moustache," said Captain Kipling.

"An American," said the parson. "How do you manage religious tolerance?"

"It's a big country," I said.

He nodded thoughtfully. "Yes, perhaps that's it."

The address Mrs. Callahan had given me over the phone was in a working-class area of Liverpool. The Callahans lived in a long row of brick-fronted houses. When I rang, Dennis's three sisters stampeded up to the door. They were short, stout girls with dark hair. Their ages ranged from fourteen to eighteen. It was a narrow little house, but comfortable. Mrs. Callahan squeezed my hand delightedly.

"What a surprise!" she said. "I can't believe you're in Liverpool. Would you like a cup of tea?"

When I said yes, the three girls galloped down the hallway to the kitchen. I was just sitting down when an elderly man entered the room.

"Da," Mrs. Callahan said kindly. "This is a friend of Dennis's. He's come all the way from the states."

"Really," snorted Grandpa Callahan. "Another bloody Yank."

As the old man glared at me, I couldn't help noticing he was missing all the fingers on his right hand and three on his left. He continued to gaze at me with bleary eyes.

"I was in the war, ya know," he said gruffly.

"World War II?" I asked.

He gave a disgruntled wave of his right stump. "World War II? How old do ya think I am?"

"Da was a pilot in World War I," Mrs. Callahan explained patiently. "His biplane was shot down."

"By Americans?" I asked, confused.

"Nay, nay, by the Gerries," Grandpa Callahan barked.

"Da's plane was on fire. A Yank pulled him out."

"So," I said, trying to understand. "That's why you don't like Americans?"

The old man scowled. "Damned Yanks!" he snorted. "How can ya pay 'em back for saving your life?"

The girls returned with a cup of strong tea and set it in front of me. I took a sip and smiled happily. It was very good.

"I didn't know if you wanted milk in your tea," offered the eldest sister. She smiled sweetly.

"This is perfect," I said. "Thanks."

The girls settled beside their mother on the sofa and gazed at me.

"So, it didn't work out in London, then?" Mrs. Callahan asked.

I told them about my experience at the Swiss Fair, even throwing in the incident at the boarding house with the towel. They all laughed heartily and the youngest sister blushed.

When I finished my tea, the girls jumped up and raced off again to the kitchen. I didn't know it, but this was the first of eight cups of tea I was to drink that day. After a while, my stomach quaked at the thought of another cup and I understood why the Callahans drank theirs with milk; it softened the bitterness.

The next morning, Mrs. Callahan glanced up from her *fry-up* of eggs, sausages, bacon, tomatoes, mushrooms, and fried bread and clapped her hands together excitedly.

"I know what you should do," she said. "You should go to the Isle of Man."

"The Isle of Man?"

"It's in the Irish Sea about halfway between Liverpool and Dublin. Douglas has a lot of hotels. They always need extra help this time of year."

"That sounds great, but …"

"I have a cousin who works at one of the hotels. I'll write you a letter of introduction."

The youngest sister was filling up my teacup for what seemed like the hundredth time that day.

"Okay," I said. "Why not?"

"Why not?" Mrs. Callahan repeated.

The ferry departed from Liverpool at eight o'clock in the evening. At the dock, Mrs. Callahan and each of her three daughters hugged me – the eldest taking an uncomfortably long time and then letting her hand brush against the front of my jeans as she stepped back. She gazed at me coyly and winked. I hoped Mrs. Callahan hadn't noticed.

As I boarded the ferry, I assumed there wouldn't be many passengers, but the ship lounges were packed. I found a seat in a forward lounge and pulled out a paperback book.

Mrs. Callahan's last words to me were, "Are you okay on ships?"

Actually, I had never been on a ship before. But why wouldn't I be okay? I'd been on motorboats many times.

"Sure," I said.

"Oh, that's fine."

Now I began to wonder. Had the Titanic sailed from Liverpool?

"Why do you ask? Is there a problem?"

She smiled encouragingly. "No, no. It's just that the Irish Sea gets a bit … um … rough at times."

I thought of this conversation now as I sat jammed together with the other passengers. The air in the lounge smelled stale and a man behind me was smoking a cigarette that put out villainous fumes. Maybe trying to read a book wasn't a good idea.

The chair in which I was sitting moved up and down with the swells. I felt queasy and walked out to the deck for fresh air. The wind blowing in off the sea was surprisingly cold and the waves were tossing. Beyond the railing was blackness. Thoughts of icebergs came to my mind, and I walked back into the lounge.

Don't try to read and you'll be fine, I told myself.

Another hour passed, and then a woman beside me opened a wicker basket and took out an egg-salad sandwich. She chomped at it noisily, and as the odor of the eggs and mayonnaise wafted over me, my stomach suddenly shifted up to my throat.

A funny thing happens to my mouth and chin when I get nauseous. The muscles in my lower lip contract, and my chin tightens as if getting ready for the worst. When this happened now, I got up and hurried out to the deck. I stood there for a long time, breathing deeply, letting the sea spray and chilly wind hit my face. The ship was scheduled to dock in Douglas at seven o'clock in the morning. It was going to be a long night. I would probably spend most of it on the deck.

As I was concentrating on breathing in and out slowly, waiting for my stomach to return to its normal position, a boy skipped toward me.

"Hello," he said cheerfully. He had chestnut brown hair and ruddy cheeks-a poster child for the classic English schoolboy.

"Hi," I said, gulping.

He looked at me for a moment. "You're not English, are you?"

I considered ignoring him, but maybe a conversation would take my mind off the swelling waves.

"No," I replied. "I'm American."

"American?" He pondered this for a time, while pushing a caramel around in his mouth with a finger. At last, he said, "My dad says Americans speak terrible English."

I wondered if he was any relation to Grandpa Callahan.

"Perhaps," I replied. "But we speak great American."

The boy looked at me. "Are you sick?"

I tried to smile. "A bit."

"A bit, yes," he murmured. "Well, goodbye."

I gave a slight nod, and he went into the lounge. I stood at the railing until I noticed an empty deck chair. It was comfortable, and I pulled the collar of my jacket around my ears. If I stayed outside on deck, I was okay. What was the cold wind compared to vomiting over the railing? The hours passed slowly and, though freezing, I slept for a while.

At daybreak, sea gulls floated in the breeze alongside the ship and an hour later we were docking at the Douglas Sea Terminal. My happiness at disembarking was tempered by the knowledge that I would have to make the return voyage in a few weeks.

The city of Douglas, nestled on the eastern coast of the Isle of Man, ran along the Bay of Douglas for about two miles. Hotels and brightly painted houses dotted the rocky coastline. The area was famous for its European motorcycle races in the summer, the Manx cat, and as the home of Richard Adams, the author of *Watership Down*.

It was a beautiful, sunny morning. Mrs. Callahan had advised me to present my letter of introduction to Mr. Stordahl at the Hotel du Man. I assumed that 7 a.m. was too early to apply for a job, so I ate breakfast and walked along the Central Promenade. At ten o'clock I entered the hotel, and within a few minutes was seated in Mr. Stordahl's office. He read the letter from Mrs. Callahan and leaned back in his chair, regarding me.

"What can you do?" he asked.

"Well," I said truthfully. "I worked a few days as a waiter in London."

"How long do you want to work here?"

"Until the end of July." I had already booked my flight home for the beginning of August.

He nodded. "All right."

Mr. Stordahl picked up his telephone. "Wait in the lobby. I'll have someone assign you a room."

An advantage to working at a hotel was that you got to live there. A maid showed me to my room on the first floor. It was large, with sunlight shining through the lace curtains of a wide window. Dropping my bag, I crawled onto the comfortable double bed. I had no idea waiters were treated so well.

Work started the next morning. I reported to the dining room in my black trousers, white shirt, and yellow jacket. Among the restaurant staff, several people attracted my interest.

The first was Patrick, a young man from Ennis in County Clare. His dark curly hair and blue eyes had the waitresses swooning, although he didn't pay them much attention. His moods shifted as quickly and randomly as clouds over Galway Bay. One moment he might be very personable, smiling, and telling jokes; the next, he would drift into a melancholy that might last days.

One afternoon we were setting tables and Patrick handed me a tray of silverware. As he reached out, his shirt cuffs slipped back. It shocked me to see slash marks on his wrists. My God, I thought, he has tried to commit suicide.

Patrick noticed me glancing at his wrists and pulled back, embarrassed.

One of the Irish waitresses told me his story. Patrick had been married to a lovely girl in Ennis and they had a baby daughter. One morning they took the child for a drive in their new Ford Capri. Patrick was driving too fast, missed a turn, and rolled the car into a field. His wife and baby were killed. He had tried to commit suicide twice since then. I had seen the scars of his last attempt.

21

How incredibly sad, I thought, to lose your young wife and child in such a tragic way.

Norah was a redhead in her early forties with an aggressive attitude. She guarded her section of the dining room with fierce possessiveness. Once I made the unfortunate mistake of serving one of her tables and from then on, she hated me.

"What's a feckin' American doin' over here, anyway?" she asked another waitress, intentionally loud enough for me to hear. "Can't get a job in his own country, I bet. Feckin' Yank."

I tried to make amends, but it was no good. Once your name was scrawled in Norah's book of grievances, you were forever labeled a *námhaid*–or enemy.

Ian was the dishwasher/poet of the hotel. He had a quiet demeanor, shoulder length hippy hair, and an affable grin. On our afternoons off, we would hike to the top of a steep hill on the south end of Douglas and look down on the city and then out to sea. Ian liked to discuss literature, and it was on one of these hikes that he mentioned Paris.

"You're so close," he said. "You should go. There's literature on every corner."

Paris, uh, I thought. I had always wanted to visit Paris, but hadn't planned on it during this trip. My original plan was to work at the Swiss Fair Restaurant in London for the summer.

"You'll never regret it," Ian urged. "You catch the ferry from Dover and then the train to Paris. It's as easy as cake."

So that put the idea of going to Paris in my mind.

I worked at the hotel for a month. What I didn't realize when Mr. Stordahl assigned me a sunny room with daily maid-service, was that the other employees lived in the basement. It was like a warren down there, dimly lit little rooms off a narrow hallway. This caused some hard feelings when they found out where I was staying. And, of course, it only increased Norah's animosity toward me.

"The feckin' American gets to live like royalty, while we live down a bloody rat's hole!"

I couldn't blame them.

On my last night in Douglas, I looked for Patrick. I had a pair of brogue shoes he liked and wanted to give them to him. As a first-time overseas traveler, I had packed twice as many things as I needed. Actually, make it four times as many things. I was tired of dragging my huge leather suitcase through airports, train stations, up gang planks, and along busy city streets and uneven sidewalks. I began to give items away and it felt wonderful. Eventually, I even gave away the suitcase and bought a smaller canvas duffle bag. What a relief. I don't know what I thinking when I packed four pairs of shoes, and enough underwear, shirts, slacks, and blue jeans to last a year. The brogues were one of my favorite pair of shoes, but I preferred to give them to Patrick than haul them around France.

He was pleased. Afterwards, I went out and walked along the promenade. Though it was midnight, the sun was still shining and people were walking and playing on the beach. I had never been to a place where the sun was still out at midnight. The beach was covered in smooth gray stones. I slipped one into my pocket as a souvenir.

As I was leaving the hotel the next morning, an ambulance screeched up to the front entrance and two medical technicians ran into the lobby. I was going to continue to the Sea Terminal until I saw them run through the door to the staff quarters in the basement.

Patrick, I thought, and hustled after them.

Most of the staff was gathered outside his door. I saw Norah with tears in her eyes.

"Is he dead?" I asked.

"No," she said. "But he's slashed his wrists again."

"I'm sorry."

"The poor lad. He's so unhappy."

I don't know which surprised me more-that Patrick had tried to kill himself or that beneath her hateful exterior, Norah had a heart.

"Is there anything I can do?" I asked.

She shook her head and turned back to the crowded doorway.

The Irish Sea was calm, and I made the return voyage to Liverpool with only a mild nausea. I didn't have time to see the Callahans again because I wanted to catch a train to London. By mid-afternoon I was at Euston Station, where I changed trains and continued to Dover. There I boarded another ferry and was soon leaning against the railing as we rumbled out to the choppy waves of the English Channel.

Those ferry crossings taught me something about myself. I learned that I absolutely loved being around ships, docks, the smell of the sea, the flutter of seagulls, and the feeling of adventure and timelessness you get when the ship moves out of port. My great-grandfather was a sea captain in Edinburgh and later Toronto. Cap Corey, they called him. However, any genetic traits I might have inherited from him had apparently diminished before I was born. My vestibular system wasn't built for a seafaring life.

Oh well, I told myself. Joseph Conrad and Jack London (among others) had already voyaged on and written about the seas. I would have to travel my own path.

Hopefully, it would be on dry ground.

On the train to Paris, I met a young chef on vacation from his job at a prominent London restaurant. Lenny was a greasy fellow with stringy hair and a bad complexion. I could picture him spending long hours working over a hot stove or frying pan. He was only stopping in Paris to visit a certain restaurant, and then he planned to take off again for Amsterdam.

"That's where all the action is," Lenny said with a lustful gleam in his eye. "Tarts in windows, drugs ... anything you want."

He rubbed his hands together in licentious anticipation and smacked his lips as if he had just tasted a good sauce.

"And restaurants?" I asked.

Lenny chuckled. "That too."

The train pulled into the Gare du Nord, and I stepped onto the platform. Paris! I could hardly believe it.

Checking into a shabby hotel, I took the Métro to the Place St. Michel. As I walked up the steps, my heart gave a leap. Around me were cafes with tables set out on the pavement, colorful tablecloths and awnings, waiters serving drinks, the fountain with sightseers gathered around it, the Seine on my left, and the smell of crepes in the air.

And wham! I was in love with the city.

I hadn't anticipated this immediate connection, this sudden emotional bonding. After all, I had not intended to visit France on this trip. It was only through the urging of a dishwasher poet on the Isle of Man that I had come. My experiences in London, Liverpool, and Douglas were merely incidents on the journey to my true destination-Paris!

I stayed in the city for five days, visiting the usual attractions, the famous cafes, plus Pablo Picasso's old studio, Ernest Hemingway's first apartment building on the rue du Cardinal Lemoine, and the shabby bookstore of Shakespeare and Company.

One afternoon I was hungry, so I bought a sandwich from a vendor on a narrow street in the Latin Quarter. At another shop I purchased a bottle of wine, and walked across the Pont Neuf to the Ile de la Cite.

At the tip of the island was the grassy Square du Vert-Galant. Sitting on a bench in the sunshine, I pulled out the sandwich. I didn't have a cup, so I uncorked the wine bottle with my army knife and took a swig.

After a few minutes, a young man came over and said something in French. I didn't understand what he wanted, so I shrugged and smiled. He studied me for a moment and then said in thickly accented English, "You are American?"

"Yes."

He looked at the wine.

"You are trying to get drunk?"

"Not really."

He smiled knowingly. "You drink from the bottle."

"I don't have a glass."

"*Ah, bon.*"

"Would you like a drink?" I asked.

"Certainly."

Tipping the bottle, he took a long chug. When he handed it back, the bottle felt considerably lighter.

"This is a Bordeaux," he mused, glancing at the label.

My knowledge of wine was limited in those days. I knew it came in red, white, and rosé. Beyond this, I was lost.

"No good?" I asked.

The young man stiffened his lower lip and shook his head slowly.

"For a sandwich, you need something lighter," he offered, pointing to my lunch. "Perhaps a Chablis."

This was my first lesson in the selection of wine.

I spent the next few days wandering the narrow streets of the Latin Quarter, Montparnasse, and Montmartre. When I finally boarded a train at the Gare du Nord for my return trip to London and flight home, I promised myself that someday I would live in Paris. And, amazingly, it wouldn't have happened except for the advice of an Irish cook on the Isle of Man, or because a Swiss restaurant manager in London had demanded I shave off my moustache.

Chapter 3
The English Language School

"Did you have any trouble finding us?" Gillian asked, showing me to a chair. "Some of these Parisian side-streets can be confusing."

"No," I replied. "I worked my way over from the Boulevard St.-Michel."

"Oh, yes. I often go that way myself," she said. "On nice days, that is."

Gillian was a tall, charming English woman with a bowl haircut and large glasses. She worked as the school secretary and assistant to Jack Duffy, the school director.

The English Language School was on a quiet side-street off the Place de l'Odeon. This was a busy commercial area only a few blocks from the Luxembourg Gardens and the Boulevard St.-Germaine. Number 12 rue de l'Odeon was the site of the original Shakespeare and Company, the famous bookstore run by Sylvia Beach. By the time I arrived in Paris–in fact, decades before I arrived in Paris-the bookstore had been moved to 37 rue de la Bûcherie, across the river from Notre Dame. George Whitman, a small man with reddish gray hair and a goatee, ran it.

Gillian smiled apologetically as she handed me a stack of forms.

"Your application was impressive," she said. "But the French government has its paperwork."

"I'm sure it has," I replied, and dug into my pocket for a pen.

I spent the next thirty minutes trying to get all the information straight while Gillian sat at her desk and glanced at me from time to time.

"I think that's it," I said, handing her the papers.

She scanned the forms.

"You've forgotten to sign page two," she commented.

I pulled out my pen again.

27

She tapped the papers against the desk. "Now we can get you in to see the boss."

Gillian showed me into a small office with a large window that overlooked an interior courtyard. Afternoon sunlight glinted through the window and across the hardwood floor.

Jack Duffy glanced up from his desk. He was a large man with unruly gray hair, a red scarf around his neck, and a gourmet's belly.

Gillian had told me his story. Jack was from Boston. After college, he joined the Navy and saved enough money to take his distraught sister on a European trip after their mother died. They had traveled around Italy, France, and Greece for several months until Jack's money ran out. His sister had returned to the states, while Jack remained in Paris and supported himself by selling newspapers on the street. Slowly, he saved enough money to start the school.

"That's quite a story," I said.

"He's a character," Gillian said.

Jack shook my hand vigorously.

"You couldn't have come at a better time," he exclaimed. "Did Gill tell you we're starting a new class next week?"

Gillian spoke up. "Afraid we haven't had time for that. I've had him filling out forms."

"I bet you're thirsty," he said. "Let's go to a café."

Leaving the school, we walked along an inner courtyard, through a short passage lined with the office windows of an architecture firm, to an outside door, and finally to the street. In addition to the multitude of narrow streets in Paris, there were also these interior walkways and passages that you couldn't always see from the outside.

Jack ordered beers at the café and I spent nearly an hour talking about my education, my teaching experience, my wife, and our reasons for being in Paris. I got the impression he was more interested in discovering who I was rather than what I'd done. I liked him immediately. He was boisterous and energetic.

"We're having a little *soiree* at the school tonight," he said, finishing his beer. "I hope you and Claudia will join us. It's a birthday party for one of the teachers."

I knew Claudia would want to meet Jack and the teaching staff. She hoped to get a part-time teaching position there herself.

"Thanks," I said. "What time?"

"Eight o'clock."

The windows of the school were brightly lit as we came up the street that evening. I felt shy about crashing a birthday party for a teacher I hadn't met, but Jack had invited us, so I opened the outer door and we stepped inside.

The party was being held in a long room with a vast table that displayed trays of cheese, caviar, fruit, roast chickens, and pastries. There were about twenty people in the room. Gillian greeted us.

"I'm so glad you could make it," she said. "I'll introduce you."

She took us around and we met the various teachers with whom I would be working. I soon discovered they all considered themselves as something else-in addition to being teachers.

For example, Gillian introduced Shauna as the poet-in-residence; Alfred was an opera singer, Mark a writer, Kelly an artist, and Susan a psychologist. Lisa was born in Italy of an American father, and Nicole was married to a Frenchman. Everyone had a story.

"And what about you?" they asked.

"Well," I said and hesitated.

"Don't tell me you're here because of Hemingway?" Mark, the writer, asked. You'd be surprised how many ..."

"No," I said. "We ..."

"Just here to see Europe?" Kelly, the artist, asked.

"Something like that," Claudia replied.

Gillian took Claudia by the elbow and guided us to the food table. It looked delicious and I was hungry. Until we got our first teaching check, we'd been trying to economize by eating only one meal a day. We had discovered a Chinese restaurant in the Marais where the appetizer, entrée, dessert, wine, and service cost the equivalent of five dollars. This was saving us money, but I could always eat more.

"Have you found an apartment?" Gillian asked.

We shook our heads.

"Hmm," she mused. "That may be a problem."

"Why?" Claudia asked.

"It's rather difficult to find one in Paris these days."

"Because they're expensive?" I asked.

"That too," she replied.

Gillian explained that when a rental apartment was advertised, people lined up outside the building before sunrise. Most times, the first person in line took the place without seeing it. They greeted the landlord with pen and checkbook in hand. It was only a question of determining how much they had to pay, and this got significantly higher every year.

"I'd like to live around here," I commented.

"Oh, the 5th arrondissement is all right," Gillian said. "But it gets rather crazy at night. You might find the 11th a better area to live … and less expensive."

"We'll check it out," Claudia said.

"The best thing is to know someone," Gillian explained. "Then you can get an apartment before it's advertised."

She gazed at us through her thick glasses. It was obvious we didn't know anyone.

"Very well," she said. "If I hear of anything, I'll let you know."

After the party we walked over to the Place St.-Michel. The area was alive with traffic, brightly lit cafes with their wine-red awnings, and the illuminated fountain. We thought about crossing over the Pont St.-Michel to the Ile de la Cite and walking around for a while, but it was nearly one o'clock and the Métro would close soon.

"I'm too tired to walk back to the hotel," Claudia said.

"Me too," I said. "Let's come back tomorrow."

She pointed to a cafe. "And let's go there. It's the epitome of what a Paris café should be – colorful, beautiful, and perfectly placed."

"Is that why you came to France?" I teased. "To find the perfect café?"

"Something like that," she replied and laughed.

In truth, we had come to France for escape–the usual American cliché. Since our arrival, though, we had learned escape took different forms; some more capricious than others; reasons that created expatriates.

After our experiences in Africa, we had found it impossible to step back into life at home. We still craved adventure, to turn our faces into the wind, to feel intense sensations.

And so, we had come to France.

"Good reason," I said.

Entering the Métro, we took out our Carte Orange tickets, passed through the turn-style, and hurried for the next train.

I had my first class the following Monday morning. The students were a group of secretaries at a large investment firm. In this job, teachers went to the various locations, rather than the students coming to the school. It was similar to the French educational system, where the teachers moved from classroom to classroom and the students remained in the same location all day.

Taking the Métro to Argentine, I came up the steps onto the Avenue de la Grande Armée. Across the street were the offices of the International Tribune, my favorite newspaper.

I was nervous as I walked into the investment company lobby and asked for directions to the conference room. I had prepared a good lesson. This was supposed to be an intermediate level class, so I planned to cover some vocabulary and then lead a directed conversation. 'Intermediate level' covered a broad range, so I wouldn't really know their levels until I evaluated their language skills.

The conference room was empty. I placed my brown leather valise on a chair and took out my lesson plans. I arranged the dry-erase board and organized the colored markers. The class was to begin promptly at ten o'clock. Eight students were scheduled to attend.

I was ready, organized, and pumped.

I waited.

And waited.

At ten minutes after the hour, two young women stuck their heads into the room and saw me seated there. One was a blonde; the other dark-haired, perhaps Spanish.

"Are you the teacher?" they asked.

I jumped up. "Yes, please come in."

They stepped into the room and took seats at the far end of the table. I got the impression that if I had moved two chairs into the hallway, they would have sat there.

Not a good sign.

"Are the others coming?" I asked.

"Others?" the blonde replied.

"There are supposed to be eight students in this class."

The dark-haired woman gave a pout. "Perhaps."

I glanced at my watch. It was now a quarter past the hour.

"Why don't we begin," I suggested. "The others can join us when they arrive."

"Very well," said the blonde.

I wrote my name on the dry-erase board and introduced myself. The two young women gazed at me with disinterest. I wondered if they were required to attend the class.

My African students had been so excited about learning, nearly falling over each other to ask and answer questions, always so happy to see me. These young women, in contrast, totally lacked enthusiasm. I pictured them looking the same way in a dentist's waiting room.

The other students never arrived.

This job was going to be difficult.

Chapter 4
The Paris-Longchamp Racecourse

It wasn't exactly true that we didn't know anyone in Paris. Claudia had a distant relative, Mary Duchêne, who had married a Frenchman many years before and now lived on the rue de Longchamp in the 16th arrondissement. This was a stylish, expensive borough of Paris.

Mary was aware we were coming to France, so shortly after our arrival, we paid her a visit. Unfortunately, she wasn't home, but her mother-in-law was available and invited us into the parlor. Madame Duchêne was in her eighties. She wore a shawl around her shoulders and walked with a cane.

Settling into a stuffed chair, she gazed at us sweetly.

"So nice to have American visitors," she said.

When she realized Claudia was a distant relative, she was even more delighted.

"Perhaps you would like something to drink?" she asked. "I can offer you orange-aid or scotch."

I chuckled and had to put a hand over my mouth.

"Orange-aid would be nice," Claudia said and gazed at me sternly. Say the wrong word, bub, and you're dead, her expression warned.

"Would you like ice?" the old woman asked.

"Yes, please," Claudia replied.

I waved a hand. "*Non, merci,*" I said. "I'm not very thirsty."

I heard a scuff of nails on the hardwood floor and a Jack Russell terrier bounded into the room. He raced around the sofa where we sat and barked furiously; loud, ear-splitting emanations that gave me an immediate headache.

"Now, now, Bruno," Madame Duchêne shouted, tapping her cane at the dog. "Silence!"

The little dog sniffed my shoe, growled, and trotted around to the back of the sofa.

"Perhaps you would like to stay for dinner?" Madame Duchêne asked.

It was only three o'clock in the afternoon.

"Thank you," Claudia said. "But we have so many things to do today."

The old woman gave a sigh and I could imagine what she was thinking. She could remember a time when duties, shopping, and meeting friends in cafes filled her days.

But now ...

Something tugged at my collar. Bruno was leaping into the air behind the sofa, trying to take little snips at my neck. I leaned forward and away from his sharp teeth.

Madame Duchêne didn't seem to notice.

As long as he's not barking, I imagined her thinking.

A few days later we visited the Duchêne's apartment again and Mary was home. She was friendly, though reserved, and we spent another afternoon in the parlor with Bruno taking stealthy nips at me. I gauged the distance between us, wondering if I could reach out and grab the little dog by the neck without Mary knowing. I was tensing for this action when a hand squeezed my wrist. Claudia gazed at me firmly. She knew exactly what I was thinking. Resigned, I leaned back into the sofa and felt the dog's hot breath once again on the back of my neck.

It was probably a good thing I didn't strangle the obnoxious little pooch, because the next week we had difficulty opening a checking account. When she heard this, Mary marched us down to the *Banque de Paris et Paye Bas* and spoke with the manager. He bowed politely and opened an account for us within minutes.

To celebrate, I suggested we stop at a café. It was a sunny afternoon and we found an outside table at the Café Kleber, up the street from Mary's apartment. Across the Trocadero were the Palais de Chaillot and the famous plaza where Adolph Hitler had stood and observed Paris after the German occupation in WWII.

Within a few minutes, it surprised me to see Madame Duchêne coming up the street. She ambled slowly along the sidewalk with her cane. When she saw us, her face brightened in greeting and I pulled up another chair.

"Ooo la," she said, daubing her cheeks with a laced hanky. "Such a lovely, warm day."

We all agreed. I asked if she would like something to drink.

"A glass of sherry, *s'il vous plaît*," she replied.

"You've been out walking?" Mary asked.

"Of course," Madame Duchêne replied with some irritation. "Why not?"

The sherry came and we all sat back and relaxed. Sunlight filtered through the horse-chestnut trees beside the café. I was excited about spending my life in such a wonderful city with such fine weather after the dry heat of Africa. I didn't realize that within a week, the weather would change and the sky become a pearl-gray blanket above our heads.

"Do you like the horse racing?" Madame Duchêne asked.

"Yes, we do," I replied.

Claudia had grown up around race horses; her father had owned five. I loved the challenge of reading the racing forms and working out the odds of which horse raced better on grass or muddy tracks, and their past performances. I never won a lot of money, but usually enjoyed an entertaining day at the track and at least broke even. (A former Irish jockey later told me all the races were fixed. I don't know if this was true, but it was still gambling on which horse would win.)

"Do you go?" Claudia asked.

Madame Duchêne gave a dismissive wave of her hand perched on top of the cane.

"No longer," she said, glancing at Mary. "But the *Prix de l'Arc de Triomphe* is coming soon. If you enjoy horse racing, you must go."

I was immediately interested.

"Where are they holding it?" I asked.

Madame Duchêne gave me a coquettish little smile. "At the Longchamp Racecourse."

The Paris-Longchamp Racecourse was a tranquil green course in the Bois de Boulogne. I had read about it and had wanted to go since we arrived in Paris.

"You should go too," Madame Duchêne said to Mary.

"Me?" Mary asked.

"*Mais oui,*" Madame Duchêne replied.

So, the following weekend, we met Mary at her apartment. She was wearing a coat because it was the first weekend in October and the weather had turned cool. I expected to see Madame Duchene in her stuffed chair and Bruno sneaking up on me from behind the sofa. Instead, the old woman's chair was empty and the terrier lay drowsily on a rug.

"He's a lot calmer today," I remarked.

"We have him on tranquilizers," Mary replied.

I glanced to see if she was joking, but she wasn't. No humor here. Bruno really was on tranquilizers. I had to suppress a grin, thinking about how the little dog must feel being drugged. He had obviously enjoyed his covert attacks on me as he sprang from behind the sofa, but now his sluggishness prevented it. Yawning, he rolled onto his side.

One of the exciting things about watching races at the Paris-Longchamp Racecourse is the natural beauty of the flowing grass circuit with the Bois de Boulogne in the background. It took me a while to get my timing down so I could study the horses as they stepped into the paddock, make my final decision, and then sprint to a betting booth.

Mary asked if I would place a few bets for her, and I did this with a mixture of curiosity and humor. Each time she placed a bet, I watched her from the corner of my eye as the horses left the post and galloped down the straightaway. Mary sat primly with her hands folded demurely in her lap. No shrill roars of excitement came from this constrained woman, no uninhibited shouts. She sat without movement and without apparent emotion–except that as the horses came around the last turn and charged toward the finish line, a thin line of perspiration appeared on her upper lip, the only sign she was emotionally engaged in the race. I imagined that if she cried out even once in excitement, the effort would crack her down the middle like a piece of Baccarat crystal.

It was a pleasant autumn afternoon with the leaves on the trees changing color and a crispness in the air. In the fourth race I won a Jumelé (paired) with horses 1 and 3, which placed 1st and 2nd and nearly stopped our hearts. It was enough to take Claudia out for dinner after we escorted Mary back to her apartment.

"She didn't like it," Claudia said as we descended the steps of the Métro Trocadero. "I didn't see her smile once."

"Oh, she liked it," I said, laughing. "But she's too sophisticated to let us know."

I told her about the fine line of perspiration erupting on Mary's upper lip each time she bet on a horse.

"Really?" Claudia asked. "I wish you'd told me. It would've been fun to see."

"Mary didn't want us to see," I said.

"So, you'll never mention it to her?" Claudia asked.

"Of course not," I replied. "I'm way too sophisticated."

"And yet you're an *American*," she noted.

"My grandfather was Canadian, if that helps."

"From the French-speaking part of Canada?"

"No. He was from Hamilton."

"Then there's no hope for you," Claudia said with a grin.

For dinner we went to a restaurant named Le Tournell off the Place St.-Michel. It was a large smoky room with wood beams and red-checkered tablecloths. On the wall below the deer heads was a shelf for napkins of the regular clients. There was no pretense about the place and the waiter was fun and had personality. We ordered roasted duck breast with asparagus, grilled potatoes, and salad washed down with a slightly chilled bottle of Red Burgundy.

As we ate, I thought about Mary Duchêne and the line of moisture on her upper lip. I wondered if she responded to other emotional incidents in the same way.

Several months after our trip to the *Prix de l"Arc de Tiomphe*, we invited Mary and her husband to our tiny flat for dinner. Claudia was an excellent cook and prepared a delicious pasta dish, but it didn't matter. Mary gazed around our shabby abode with obvious disgust, quietly picked at her dinner, and left.

We never heard from her again.

"It must've been the cork," Claudia offered.

One leg of our dining table was short, so I had propped it up with a wine cork. Twice during the dinner, I had to adjust the cork so the table didn't wobble. We were used to this, but apparently it didn't impress the Duchênes.

"I guess they thought we had more money," I offered.

"I expected Mary to be more forgiving," Claudia said. "She is, after all, distant family."

"I'll miss the dog."

Claudia laughed. "I forgot about Bruno."

"Not me," I said, remembering his teeth snapping within a millimeter of my neck. "I can still feel his doggy breath on my collar."

"He's on tranquilizers now," she said.

"Weird that he only went for me."

"He knows a gauche American when he sees one," she said and laughed again.

"And I've worked so hard," I said.

Chapter 5
At the Hotel with Saleem & Said

During the weeks we stayed at the Deux Hemispheres Hotel, I became good friends with the two Algerian desk clerks Saleem and Said. Their names fit their personalities perfectly, because in Arabic, Saleem means tranquil and Said means happy. You could not have chosen two more appropriate descriptions. Saleem was introspective and enjoyed playing chess and discussing politics. Said was a natural born comedian and could make anything funny.

Once we got to know them, they often invited us to dine with them in the hotel lounge. Invariably, these dinners consisted of couscous and chicken, couscous and rabbit, or couscous and vegetables. While we ate, Said would entertain us with exaggerated imitations of French manners or by pretending to be a proper French Madame. We would fall out of our chairs laughing.

One evening while we were dining, one of the two Algerian cleaning women came into the lounge. This was Sadia, whose husband had remained in Algiers. I knew this because she had shown me his photograph. The faded sepia portrait looked like those taken in West Africa. The man gazing sternly from its scratched image appeared years older than Sadia. I wondered if theirs had been an arranged marriage.

When she came into the lounge, Sadia was carrying a small blue sweater. She held it out to Said.

"I found this in the dryer," she explained in French.

Said held up the sweater, turning it from side to side.

I imagined it belonged to a boy of about nine or ten. It was about that size.

"I don't recall any boys staying in the hotel," he mused. "Perhaps…"

43

He stopped talking and gazed at the label. His eyes widened and his mouth opened.

"No," he exclaimed. "It's not possible."

"What?" I asked.

He held the label between thumb and first finger.

"This is *my* size, but ..."

"It's yours?" I asked.

A slow rumble of laughter emitted from him. It increased until his face was red and he held a hand to his eyes.

"It is mine!" he blurted. "How is this possible? It is so small!"

"The dryer," I said. "It shrank."

"But my god," he said. "A child could wear it!"

He gazed at Sadia. "Do you know any boys?"

She nodded.

"Then it's yours," he said and tossed it to her.

Sadia took the sweater and walked back to the office.

Said shook his head slowly.

"I liked that sweater," he said.

Then his mouth began to twitch, and we both laughed again.

One evening when we returned to the hotel, Said pulled me aside. He looked perplexed.

"What's wrong?" I asked.

"Those women," he said, motioning to a group of older women seated at a table in the lounge. "I can't tell where they are from?"

"Don't you have their passports?"

He raised his sharp nose toward a plump woman on the left. "Hers, yes, but the others ... no."

"Ask them," Claudia suggested.

"It is too embarrassing," he said. "I cannot even tell what language they are speaking."

"Maybe I can help," I said.

Ambling over to a table near the women, I sat down and pretended to read a copy of Le Monde. I listened to them talking for a minute and shrugged. Said was right. I had no idea what language they were speaking. Perhaps Norwegian or Swedish.

"Let me try," Claudia said.

She sat near the women for a few minutes and then leaned over and began chatting with them. She pointed to me and they all laughed.

"How can she do that?" I asked Said.

"You are asking me?" he said, perplexed. "She is your wife."

Claudia returned to the counter.

"How did you do that?" I asked.

She laughed. "They're from Scotland. They're speaking English."

"I didn't understand a word," I protested.

"It's the accent, not the words," she said.

Said burst into laughter. "They are speaking *your* language, and *you* didn't understand?"

He slapped me on the back.

"Shut up," I said.

On another evening, I was playing chess with Saleem in the hotel lobby when Claudia burst in from the street. She had visited Lena Allard and her dark eyes sparkled merrily.

"Lena says they might have an apartment for us," Claudia announced.

We had been looking for an apartment every day, but with no luck. Every place we heard about was snatched up before we could get there. We just weren't fast enough. As Gillian had said, we needed to hear about an apartment *before* it was advertised. Maybe our luck had changed.

"Great," I said. "Where is it?"

"On the rue des Trois Couronnes. Near the Boulevard de Belleville."

I didn't know this quarter, but it didn't matter.

"How much is the rent?" I asked.

We were on a tight budget and I didn't want her to get excited about a place we couldn't afford, although she knew our finances as well as I did.

Claudia slid onto a chair next to me. Saleem looked up from the chessboard and rested his chin on his hands, impatient to continue.

"No rent," she replied. "Isn't that amazing?"

"No rent?" I asked. "What's the catch?"

She clapped her hands. "Lena said we could live there if we do two little things."

"Uh huh?"

"First, I have to help her renovate two apartments they bought in the Marais."

"That's something you wanted to do anyway, isn't it?"

"Yes," she said.

Since there was a finite amount of living space in Paris, younger residents were required to either purchase houses in the surrounding villages–pushing farther and farther out until they reached the last stop of the RER–or they purchased something within the city. Since real estate prices in Paris were astronomically high, many buyers bought tiny apartments that required work.

Lena and her husband had a small business where they bought decrepit old apartments in the Marais and renovated them for sale or rent. The Marais was a fashionable area in the 4th Arrondissement that had once been the city's Jewish quarter. When I say old, we're talking 17th century, though you wouldn't know that by looking at them. Over the decades, the walls and ceilings had been covered with a mélange of particle board or sheet rock, destroying the original charm of the rooms.

Lena's plan was to strip the old interiors down to their original plaster walls and beams, put in new tile floors, update the wiring and plumbing, and voila! Have a charming apartment for sale. They made a hefty profit from renovating and flipping these old places, and planned to retire in a few years to the south of France.

Claudia would have helped them for free. Turning a dilapidated Paris hovel into a charming new residence was work she enjoyed. She found the technical side of renovating challenging and exciting.

"And the second thing?" I persisted.

"We can only stay three months," she replied. "Then they're going to renovate it."

"Three month's free rent," I said. "That should give us plenty of time to find a place."

"That's what I was thinking," she said.

Saleem glanced up from the chessboard in surprise. "You are leaving?"

Chapter 6
Rue des Trois Couronnes

We met Lena the next morning on the rue des Trois Couronnes, a narrow cobble-stoned street lined with apartment buildings painted in washed-out pastels. On the corner were three cafes, a pastry shop, a vegetable stand, and a shoe repair. The local residents were a mixture of Algerian, Russian, African, and Portuguese–a real working-man's quarter. At the rotisserie grill, three goat heads turned slowly on spits.

"Oh, yum," Claudia said and covered her mouth.

Trois Couronnes (Three Crowns) was a pretentious name for the little street with its crumbling old buildings. To enter number 10, we pushed open a heavy wooden door and stepped into the courtyard.

"Don't be put off by the looks," Lena warned. "You know this is temporary. Nicolas believes another apartment will become available soon."

"How soon?" I asked.

"In a few months."

"We're happy to have this one," Claudia said.

We passed the ground-floor apartment of a man playing the piano. A worn, circular stairway led up to the third floor. On the landing of each floor, was an ancient toilet that reeked of urine and human waste.

"Gees," I muttered as we passed the second toilet and I nearly gagged. "How many rats died in there?"

"Don't be negative," Claudia said.

When we reached the third floor, we walked down an open balcony to the apartment door.

"*Eh voila,*" Lena said.

A large window on our right was open, and I could hear the chatter of children and smell fish and garlic. We could also hear a woman's raised voice.

"Spanish?" I asked Lena.

"Portuguese," she whispered.

I felt as if we were being watched and glanced up to the fourth-floor railing. A man with wild hair and a crazed look in his eyes stood there. He gazed at us without moving.

"*C'est le fou,*" Lena whispered again, unlocking the door. "It's best to ignore him."

We entered the apartment, which was basically two rooms. The first was a combination kitchen and bathroom. The bathroom was about the size of a telephone booth with a toilet and a stand-up shower. The bathroom sink was *in* the shower. While seated on the toilet, your knees stuck into the kitchen, and you couldn't close the door. The wallpaper was peeling and the place smelled dank.

The second room was a bedroom with a large wooden bed frame that nearly touched the walls on either side. Two large shuttered windows looked onto the rue Jean Pierre, a pleasant street with shops and cafes.

Lena gazed at us. "I know it isn't what you wanted, but ..."

"It's perfect," I said.

"Wonderful!" Claudia exclaimed.

We moved out of the Deux Hemispheres Hotel two days later. As we piled our bags into a taxi, Salim and the two femmes des ménage-Sadia and Monica-came out to the sidewalk. They stood shoulder to shoulder and waved tearfully as we drove away.

"Come back anytime," Salim called.

"We will," I shouted and waved.

We needed a mattress for the large bedframe, so Lena gave us the names of several places. We eventually found one at the Marché de Clignancourt. The difficulty was getting the large awkward thing back to our apartment on the Métro. We were like a vaudeville comedy team carrying it down the Métro stairs, through the turn-style, and onto the coach. Fortunately, heavy plastic wrapping kept the mattress from getting dirty.

When we reached our building, we hauled the mattress up the dark smelly stairs to our third-floor apartment. Finally, we slid it onto the bed frame and stood back, gasping.

"We live in Paris," I said happily.

"Yes, we do," Claudia said and let out a sigh.

Within a few weeks of tramping up and down the stairs as I headed to work, the market, or out for a walk, I got to know the residents of the apartments opening onto the interior courtyard. The woman I had heard shouting at her children was part of a Portuguese family named Carvalho that lived in the apartment next to ours. Amazingly, a father, mother, three children, and a grandmother all lived in the studio apartment and slept in the same room. I marveled as I passed their window and heard them singing or laughing together. The father's name was Miguel. The mother, Sofia, brought us a pot of Portuguese stew. It was thick with vegetables, potatoes, and pork-stuffed sausages. We ate it with a warm baguette, dipping the bread in olive oil, and it was delicious.

When Miguel made a trip to Villa Nova de Gaia, he returned with a bottle of Mateus–a medium-sweet Portuguese rosé wine. He poured me a glass and I sipped at it tentatively; it was *frizzante*, and I'm not much of a rose drinker. But after one swallow, I could have easily chugged the bottle.

The man on the ground floor with the piano was a music teacher. A hand-printed sign advertising PROFESSEUR DE MUSIQUE sat in his window. I never spoke with him, but he was often giving lessons at his piano as I passed, tapping out time by smacking the flat of his palm against his knee. He wore an old sweater and needed a haircut. A variety of worn furniture–no doubt from thrift shops, filled his apartment. I felt sorry for him. This was the bottom rung of the music business; teaching unmotivated students in a ground floor studio of a déclassé neighborhood. I doubted he had planned to end up like this in the early days, when his heart burned with a passion for music.

Then there was the 'spook' on the fourth floor. I often saw him as I came and went from our apartment. He seemed to always be leaning against the railing and watching. I guessed he was probably in his early thirties. He spoke, but watched intently. He gave us all the creeps – especially Claudia.

"He's always watching me," she said. "If he ever comes down to our floor, I'm gonna freak."

I didn't get the impression *le fou* was dangerous, but he certainly was creepy. When the Allards bought his apartment and forced him to move, they discovered he was, among other things, a hoarder.

Nicolas came to our door.

"Do you want to see something incredible?" he asked.

We followed him upstairs.

"Stand back," he said and opened *le fou's* door. Or rather, he opened it a crack and then put his shoulder to it.

The door opened enough for us to see that the entire apartment was full of junk. It filled the rooms from the floor up to within two feet of the ceiling.

Nicolas pointed to the narrow gap.

"That's where he lives," he said. "He crawls up there and sleeps on a piece of cardboard."

"Can you imagine?" Claudia murmured.

"What does he eat?" I asked.

Nicolas gazed at me. "Do you really want to know?"

"Maybe not," I said.

"Good," he said. "Because I don't wish to throw up again."

It took the Allards three weeks to remove all the junk from *le fou's* apartment. Mice, cockroaches, and spiders infested the place.

I eventually learned what he ate when I discovered a metal pan containing the bones of a cooked rat and pigeon feathers. There was also something that might have been worms, but I didn't look closely.

It shocked me that anyone could live this way. I also was concerned that the infested apartment was only one floor above and across the courtyard from ours.

"It's inhuman," Claudia said with a shiver.

"Look on the bright side," I said. "You get to help renovate it."

"Guess who's going to help me?" she asked.

"Lena?"

Claudia gazed at me, shook her head, and smiled.

"When do we start?" I asked.

Initially, Claudia promised to help Lena on Mondays and Wednesdays–a workable schedule with her part-time teaching duties. But soon she was spending every free minute in the Marais, learning about renovating, how to cut tile, and the intricacies of plumping. She would assist Lena with the wiring–something at which Claudia was especially adept–and then meet me at a café for lunch. The more dust she had on her cheeks and in her hair, the happier she appeared. She was delighted and so was I, as it gave her something to do after two years of isolated existence in Africa.

I often wondered what she might find inside those old 17th century walls; a rusted dueling pistol, perhaps, or a sword?

A friend who knew of my interest in writing came up with the most imaginative idea.

"What if Claudia discovers a mysterious suitcase?" my friend suggested. "And inside are Hemingway's lost early stories ... the ones stolen from Hadley on the train. And she brings them to you and ..."

I thought about this idea for a long time. It was even better than finding a pearl-handled dueling pistol or a copy of Le Figaro from 1826.

Alas, she only found ancient spider webs.

Chapter 7
Doc Watson in Paris

"There they are," Claudia said.

We sat on the terrace of a café near the International Refugee School. Claudia was now teaching there two days a week. I gazed across the crowded Boulevard de Capucines and saw a young couple strolling toward us. It was a cool evening and the young woman had pulled her fur-lined collar around her ears. She was small, with a round face and beautiful long brown hair. The young man was tall and thin with blond hair and a peaked nose. She looked Slavic. He looked German. These were Tanya and Peter-Czech refugees Claudia had met at the school.

"You can't imagine how much they know about bluegrass music," she said as they came up the sidewalk. "It's incredible."

I wondered how two Czechs could know so much about this very specific type of American music. I was showing my ignorance here, not realizing bluegrass music was popular in Czechoslovakia, and in some ways, had originated in the country.

Claudia made the introductions and we ordered drinks.

"How long have you been in Paris?" I asked.

This was a standard question and told you a lot about a person. How long they had been living in Paris was everything, so to speak.

Tanya glanced at Peter.

Had I asked a troubling question?

"For me, a month," she replied. "For Peter, two weeks."

"You didn't come together?"

"No," Peter replied. "We came separately. Though not because we wanted to."

Tanya shook her dark hair. "Never because we wanted to."

A waiter brought the drinks and set them on our small table. I held up my beer.

"Welcome to Paris," I said.

We clinked glasses.

Tanya took a sip of her wine and set down the glass.

"You want to know about us?" she asked seriously.

"Only if you want to talk about it," I replied.

"We *need* to talk about it," Peter said. "We want people to understand."

"Because it's not just about the music," Tanya offered.

Peter grinned. He had a broad, infectious grin.

"It's not *only* about the music," he said.

I had heard of Alexander Dubček's attempts to make Czechoslovakia a more democratic country; the result being that awful day in August, 1968, when Soviet tanks rolled across the border and into Prague. The months of protest leading up to the Warsaw Pact invasion were known as the Prague Spring.

When you hear about sweeping political events in other countries, one has–or at least *I* had–a tendency to think in terms of national events. I didn't give much thought to how it affected individual people. However, as I was to learn, the Soviet invasion dramatically altered the lives of Peter and Tanya.

It began, ironically, with music.

Peter's father, Marek Bressler, was a violinist in the Prague Symphony. He was also a member of a clandestine group that met weekly and discussed political reform. When the Warsaw Troops invaded Czechoslovakia on August 20, Marek was performing with the symphony in London. As he was boarding a plane at Heathrow Airport for his return flight, Bressler was warned he would be arrested upon his arrival in Prague. Someone from the discussion group had informed on him. When the plane touched down at Charles de Gaulle Airport in Paris, he had claimed asylum, stayed in France, and eventually settled in Provence.

Peter's school expelled him when his father defected. The communist government had no interest in educating the children of defectors. Unable to continue his education, he apprenticed as a machinist. On his eighteenth birthday, he received papers for his "universal military obligation" to the Russian army. Young Czechs were drafted and shipped off to fight in Afghanistan. Peter put off his inscription for as long as possible.

He met Tanya Bartošová at a party. They hit it off immediately and were soon talking about emigrating. Peter didn't want to join the army, and Tanya wanted the freedom to make her own life choices. They spent months planning their escape and decided she would go first. It was too risky for them to be seen on the train together. Instead, Tanya's cousin Edvard offered to escort her on the journey. He also wanted to avoid the draft.

On the evening of her escape, Tanya kissed her younger sister Mila goodnight. Then she quietly grabbed her bags. She hadn't been able to tell Mila she was leaving because her sister might inadvertently mention it to someone. Informers were everywhere. Many young Czechs were trying to get out of Prague and the police were cracking down. After hugging her weeping parents, Tanya tread quietly down the stairs and out to the darkened street. She didn't know if she would ever see her family again.

Edvard was waiting for her at the train station. They boarded the same coach, but did not sit together. As the train approached the German border, Czech police came down the aisle and demanded to see papers. Tanya and Edvard had forged documents. The police thought Edvard's papers were suspicious and hauled him off the train. They weren't concerned with Tanya. So, shaking and in tears, she continued to France alone.

When she reached Paris, Tanya found her way to a Métro station and boarded a train. She had the address of a distant friend who could give her a place to stay. After a few stops, a Métro agent came through the car and asked to see her ticket. Tanya had never been on a Métro before and didn't have a ticket. Nor could she understand what the man was saying in French. When he escorted her off the train, she broke down, believing they were sending her back to Prague. Eventually, the agent released her with a warning and Tanya made her way to the safe-haven address.

For the next week, she went to the station each afternoon and watched as passengers disembarked from the Prague train. No Peter. She had nearly given up hope, afraid he had been arrested or changed his mind, when he stepped onto the platform.

Now that they were both safely in Paris, their goal was to reach the United States. They spoke a little English, but not enough for them to feel comfortable, or to understand the lyrics of their favorite bluegrass guitarist and singer, Doc Watson. They signed up for language classes at the refugee school, and this is where they met Claudia.

"Now you know about us," Tanya said, her soft brown eyes suddenly intense.

I pictured Tanya kissing her younger sister goodbye, knowing she might never see Mila again. I tried to imagine how much courage this would take, how much determination; and that it wasn't a romanticized story like you might read in a novel, but a true, harsh reality.

"You see, it's not just about the music," Peter added. "It's about freedom."

"I understand," I said.

"You're so brave," Claudia said.

"One more thing," Tanya spoke up.

"What?" I asked.

She gazed at us. "All Russians should be killed like *dogs*!"

The pronouncement sounded so hateful spoken in her thick Czech accent. Her words hung in the cool Parisian air–quivering with rage and sorrow–and then drifted away as we moved on to their love of Doc Watson.

Later, I thought about Tanya and Peter and their experiences in getting across the border to Germany and finally, France. Sometimes when you're young, you're able to achieve incredible things, to overcome amazing obstacles, because in your eagerness and innocence, you aren't aware of the hindrances. Or if you are, you believe you will succeed because there is something special about you.

Gandhi wrote, "Man often becomes what he believes himself to be."

Tanya had this belief in herself as she packed her bags that evening in Prague and prepared to slip out of the country. Since that warm August night when Russian tanks rolled into the city and took over the Czech government, the lives of Peter and Tanya had been on this trajectory. The incident known as the Prague Spring had altered their destinies.

Chapter 8
Life with Hailey

"I think these will fit you," Hailey said, handing Claudia a pile of skirts, blouses, and sweaters.

"Oh, please," Claudia protested. "I can't take all of this."

"Doubt you'll find many things that fit you in Paris," Hailey said. "French styles aren't made for girls like us."

She was referring to the perfect French model body: slender, petite, and as fine-boned as a bird. I had seen some of these young women promenading along the Place Vendôme.

"I can't ..." Claudia began, but Hailey cut her off.

"You'd be doing me a favor. Everyone who leaves Paris gives me their clothes. My closet is full." She laughed delightedly. "Girls ... that is."

If the Place de l'Odeon was the geographic spindle around which we turned in Paris, Hailey Barrow was the social spindle around which our lives revolved. She was the center of everything, knew everyone, had helped nearly everyone, and was an important resource for almost everything a person wanted to do or needed to know about living in France.

Like so many other people we'd met in Paris, Hailey was a curious mixture of personality traits–amazingly generous in some situations and dismissive in others. She never hesitated to help friends in need, and yet, after offering help, she lost respect for them because they had required her assistance. The best way to maintain a friendship with Hailey, I realized, was to never ask her for anything. In this way, she admired you.

We met her through mutual friends, and she was immediately friendly. She lived in an apartment at 17 rue de Malte, near the Métro Oberkampf. It was only a few blocks from the Place de la Republique and close to several good cafes, a wine shop, a butcher shop, and a bakery. The first time we dropped by her second-floor apartment, she offered us wine, cheese, and advice. Then she studied Claudia's attire and walked into the bedroom. When she came out, her arms were full of clothes.

Claudia picked out a few blouses and two sweaters. We left with the promise that we would return in a few weeks for Hailey's first big party of the year.

As we stepped out to the street, I stood for a moment and gazed up at the apartment building. There was something about the place and the little square on the corner that was incredibly charming.

"I wish we could live here," I said wistfully.

Claudia glanced up at the windows with their open shutters.

"I don't think my closet is large enough," she said, and we both laughed.

Still, as we crossed the street toward the Métro, I couldn't help but wonder if it was possible.

On the evening of Hailey's party, <u>We Will Rock You</u> by Queen was playing as we came up the stairs. She greeted us at the door, giving us kisses on both cheeks. A martini balanced precariously in her hand.

"I'm so glad you're here," she said. "Drinks and snacks are over there. Have fun."

Then she was gone, flitting away with the other guests.

Claudia and I stood in the doorway for a moment, dazzled, and then worked our way over to the drink table.

As the evening progressed and <u>We Will Rock You</u> gave over to <u>We Are the Champions</u>, I met a variety of artists, writers, poets, teachers, and drifters.

At one point, I encountered two young women from Spain.

"My name is Carmen," one of them said. "This is my cousin. We're from Alicante."

"Hello," said the cousin with a shy smile.

"And what's your name?" I asked her.

"Carmen," she replied.

I was confused. I had guzzled several pints of beer by this time. Perhaps I had misunderstood.

"Isn't *your* name Carmen?" I asked the first young woman.

"Yes," she replied. "And so is my cousin. We are both named Carmen."

"So ... you're both from Alicante ... you're cousins ... and you're both named Carmen?"

"*Si, si,*" they said and hugged each other.

"What're the odds," I said.

Next, I met an English railway worker from London. Tony was tall, thin, wore a droopy moustache, wire-rimmed glasses, and had a star earring in his left ear. He was a member of the Communist Party and told me how they were attempting to organize left-wing groups in the United States. His conversation reminded me of the strange man I'd met at the Regent's Park Hotel in London so many years ago. Tony said he was only at Hailey's party for a few hours because he had to catch a train to Italy that evening.

I noticed a guitar pin on his vest.

"You're a musician?" I asked, trying to change the subject from politics.

"Oh yeah, mate," he said. "I play rhythm guitar and some piano ... chords mostly."

"Sounds like fun," I said.

Tony's eyes lit up. "Presently, I'm trying to set *Mein Kampf* to music."

"*Mein Kampf?*" I asked. "You mean Hitler's manifesto?"

"That's the one," he replied with a grin. "Bit of a challenge."

"I can imagine," I said.

It was around 2 am when Hailey suggested we all go for a drive in her new BMW. The car had just been delivered that afternoon and she was excited to test it out in Paris.

"You mean now?" I asked.

"No, no," she laughed. "In the morning. Will you come?"

Claudia shrugged. She wasn't much interested in cars. She let me know this was my decision.

I loved BMWs and had always wanted one. I could see myself racing down the German Autobahn in my sleek BMW E30, wearing soft leather driving gloves and reflective sunglasses, while Beethoven's Fifth Symphony thundered on the radio. That was driving!

"Sounds like fun," I said.

We arrived at 17 rue de Malte late the next morning, still partially hung-over from the party. Hailey had developed an exciting plan. We would not only ride around Paris but also go for a drive in the countryside. My stomach was still feeling queasy. I didn't know if I wanted to spend the morning zooming around curves on narrow farm roads.

"We'll think about it," I said.

"Oh, c'mon," she insisted. "It'll be fun."

"Not too far," Claudia said.

Hailey thought for a moment, and her face brightened. "We'll take a picnic lunch! I have wine, cheese, olives, and pate from the party. We can pick up a fresh baguette at the boulangerie."

She parked her new BMW on the street. If she had lived up near the Boulevard de Rochechouart, the hubcaps and wheels would have been stolen by now—possibly even the car itself. A friend once stopped at a red light in that quarter. While he was waiting, two boys stole his rear hubcaps. When he got out to chase them, two other boys stole his front hubcaps. He was lucky to get away without losing anything else.

"You're not going to park it on the street every day, are you?" I asked.

"No," she replied. "I've rented a garage space."

"Good," I said. "Because you know ..."

"I know," she said. "But I'm not keeping the car anyway. I'm sending it home in a few months."

"To Seattle?"

She nodded.

Hailey put on her sunglasses and climbed into the driver's seat. Claudia got into the back.

"Wouldn't you like to sit up front?" I asked.

"Oh, no," she said. "I'll stay back here where it's safe."

I took the passenger seat and off we went.

There were two things I hadn't considered about driving with Hailey. First was that she didn't know how to drive a stick-shift car. Second was that she barely knew how to drive any car very well, no matter what the shift.

We slammed up the Boulevard Voltaire at a frightening speed with Hailey changing lanes at random, screeching around curves and nearly going airborne when we hit the Boulevard St.-Martin. In all that time, I don't think she was ever out of second gear.

"Shift!" I cried. "You've got to shift!"

"Oh, right," she yelled as we barely missed an approaching bus.

Jamming down the clutch, she crunched the gear-shift, first pressing the stick this way and then that–listening to the gears grinding and then catching. She didn't know if she was in third gear or fifth. I sucked in my breath, appalled at what she was doing to her precision car.

It wasn't until we reached the Arc de Triomphe that I wondered if we were going to survive the morning. The motto for Parisian drivers is: *drive twice as fast as you think possible, and imagine your car is half the size it really is.*

Recently, a driver had slammed into an elderly pedestrian on the Avenue D'Italie and continued for twenty minutes with the poor man's dead body on the roof of the car.

The circle around the Arc was a demolition derby on any morning, with cars careening at you from every possible direction. I'd driven around it before with spotters on either side yelling, "INCOMING RIGHT! INCOMING LEFT!"

Now Hailey was driving as if her BMW was the only car in Paris. If she had reached over to casually adjust her car radio, I wouldn't have been surprised.

"Ah!" Claudia screamed when a truck entering the circle from the Avenue Hoche nearly rammed into us.

"Get us out of here!" I yelled, with a driver so close beside us I could almost smell his breath.

Hailey spun the wheel and we catapulted down the Avenue Victor Hugo. I'm sure she was still in second gear. After two blocks, she whipped into a parking space at the curb and leaned back in her seat.

"Wow!" she exclaimed.

My hands were shaking. I glanced at Claudia. She appeared to be frozen with her mouth ajar.

"Exciting, huh?" Hailey asked. "I think this sweetie handles pretty well in traffic."

"Yeah," I said, breathing out slowly.

"Driving in the country should be easier," she said.

"Where are we going?" Claudia asked. She had become unfrozen.

"I was thinking Giverny," Hailey replied, adjusting the rearview mirror.

Claude Monet's house and gardens were in Giverny. Monet was my favorite artist. I wanted to visit his house and see the water-lily pond – but not today.

"I thought we weren't going that far," Claudia said.

"We'll drive for a while and then stop for our picnic, okay?" Hailey asked, already stomping on the accelerator.

Before I could reply, we shot down the avenue toward the Bois de Boulogne. Within thirty minutes, we were on a narrow country road lined with poplar trees and open fields. The car's engine clanked and hot steam poured from beneath the hood.

"Oh, no," Claudia muttered.

The engine died and we rolled to a stop.

"What happened?" Hailey asked. "I thought Beemers were good cars."

"I don't think you ever got out of second gear," I offered.

"This is such an inconvenience," she sighed.

A road sign ahead announced that Rambouillet was two kilometers away.

"We could have our picnic here," Hailey suggested. "I'm getting hungry."

"Let's deal with the car first," I said.

The weather was cool and the sky clear; no rain clouds on the horizon. We began to walk. I enjoyed listening to the wind rustling the poplar leaves over our heads and blowing across the tall grass in the fields. We were about halfway to Rambouillet when a young man in a Land Rover pulled up.

"Was that your BMW back there?" he asked.

"Hers," I said, pointing to Hailey.

"Can you take us to a garage?" she asked.

"Certainly," he replied.

Hailey spent thirty minutes discussing repairs with a Rambouillet auto mechanic. He said the work would take at least two days, depending on if he had to order parts. So, we asked for directions to the local *gare* and caught a train back to Paris.

As we rolled along the tracks, Hailey gazed at us.

"You two were so calm," she said. "You never got angry. I really appreciate it."

I glanced at Claudia and she grinned. We had recently moved to Paris from the savannahs of West Africa where almost nothing worked properly. Breaking down for an hour in a BMW on a beautiful French country road was no big thing. We had done it frequently in the region around Pindjali–and in 120-degree heat.

"Piece of cake," I muttered.

"With cherries," Claudia replied.

We didn't hear from Hailey for several weeks. During this time, Lena Allard arrived at our door and said we had to move. She and Nicolas were going to start renovating the apartment on Monday. It was now Saturday. This was our agreement when we moved into Trois Couronnes. The Allards had allowed us to stay without paying rent, but we had to move when the renovation began.

When Lena left, Claudia turned to me. Her face was ashen.

"We've looked and looked," she said, nearly in tears.

"Something always comes through for us," I said, giving her a hug. "I can't help thinking it'll happen again."

"Better hurry," she said, wiping her eyes.

We began the tedious job of piling clothes and dishes into boxes. Our nerves were on edge and we snapped at each other. In the damp night streets, I was out again, searching for more boxes.

On Sunday morning, Peter and Tanya came over to help us carry our luggage down to the street. Salim was waiting in his car to transport our things back to the Deux Hemispheres Hotel. We would soon be back to where we had started. Claudia rode ahead with Salim while I secured the windows and locked the apartment.

I was just closing the door for the last time when Sofia Carvalho leaned out of her window.

"A call for you," she said, smiling.

The Carvalho's had a telephone and we had given out their number in case of emergencies. This was the first time anyone had called us.

"May I come in?" I asked.

"*Si, si,*" she said.

It was Hailey.

"Natalie is moving out upstairs," she said. "The landlady is here now. I think if you hurry, you can rent it."

Natalie was a French girl who lived on the third floor at 17 rue de Malte. The very apartment building I wanted to live in. It couldn't be true.

Fewer Métro trains ran on Sundays and I didn't want to waste time in the station, so I raced down the stairs and out to the street. I ran around the corner to the rue Jean-Pierre, full out along the Avenue Parmentier, and finally down to the rue Oberkampf.

I could hardly breathe by the time I reached the rue de Malte, but I hurried up the stairs with checkbook in hand.

Hailey had buzzed me in and stood in her open doorway as I passed.

"Good luck," she called.

As I ascended the third-floor staircase, my mind raced with questions. What if someone else was already interested in the apartment? Would the proprietor want to rent to Americans? What should I say to her in French?

Fortunately, Natalie had paved the way by telling the landlady about us.

Madame Bardin was a short, plump, older woman with brassy red hair. She had formerly been a *femme de ménage,* but had injured herself on the job and used the compensation money to buy this apartment. She nodded her approval and I wrote out a check.

The place was ours!

Claudia was so excited she was practically dancing. She wanted to know everything Madame Bardin had told me.

"Can we go back right now?" she asked. "I want to see the place and see how our furniture will fit."

This time we didn't have to run.

Later we went out to dinner and it began to rain, so we hailed a taxi back to the hotel.

Gazing through the rain-streaked taxi window as we sped along the Cours de la Reine, I saw the Eiffel Tower looming vast and gray across the river. Then we passed the Place de la Concorde with its myriad of round white street lamps that resembled fire-flies hovering above a frosted field, and the Jardin des Tuileries—so dark and lonely in the rain.

Salim was seated at a table in the hotel dining room as we entered. He was studying a newspaper.

"What are you doing?" I asked.

He held up the paper. "*Dimanche Turf*," he said. "I'm choosing my horses for Auteuil."

I grinned. "What do you always ask me to bring you?"

He scratched the back of his head thoughtfully, and then his dark eyes lit up.

"Champagne!" he cried.

"Champagne it is," I said, and pulled a bottle from beneath my coat.

"It's time to celebrate," Claudia said. "We really live in Paris now."

As we sipped the champagne, cold and *pétillant* in our throats, I thought about how close we had come to not getting an apartment in Paris, and how Hailey Barrow had saved us with that last-minute phone call. I didn't give a damn anymore about how poorly she drove, or that she had some unusual friends—including one who wanted to put *Mein Kampf* to music. Hailey had helped us and I would be forever grateful. Sometimes she lost respect for friends she had assisted, but I hoped this wasn't true for us. After all, she had helped herself in a way, because we were now her neighbors. And who wouldn't want us for neighbors?

Interestingly, on that first walk-through of our new apartment, Claudia lingered in the bedroom for several minutes, checking the armoire's size for her clothes.

Chapter 9
The Flea Circus

A flea was crawling up my leg. I sat across the desk from Ruben Fayolle, assistant director of one of France's largest insurance companies. Monsieur Fayolle had hired me to help him with his English. As part of the job, I was required to wear a sport coat and tie so that I fit into the corporate image; just another executive.

I found it amusing and didn't mind putting on a tie twice a week. Working with Monsieur Fayolle, however, was not enjoyable. He bore a striking resemblance to Humphrey Bogart–if Bogart was anorexic. He had an extremely high opinion of himself and his position, demonstrated by the soccer field of mahogany desktop that separated us in his office.

Considering the man's lofty position and that I was there to teach him English, it didn't help that I had a flea crawling up my leg. It was more than disconcerting. It was torture. I could feel the little bugger meandering its way up from my sock to my knee. I nonchalantly dug at it with a finger, but you can't kill them that way. Fleas are extremely tough. The only way I'd found to kill one was to squeeze it between my thumb and index finger, hold it down to a hard surface, and crush it with a fingernail. Simply squeezing wouldn't do–it was necessary to crunch their hard bodies.

My problem with fleas had begun a week earlier when we moved into our apartment on the rue de Malte. In every respect we loved the place–except for one. The previous tenant had owned cats, and the place was infested. There was no bedframe in the bedroom, so we had put our mattress on the floor. I don't know if this made us more accessible to the fleas, but during the night I felt something crawling on me.

"There's something in the bed," I whispered to my wife. "Do you feel anything?"

She yawned. "Like what?"

"Something crawling."

She rolled onto her side. "Bed bugs?" She hated bed bugs.

"Don't think so."

"Good," she said and closed her eyes.

I tried to close my eyes too, but a few minutes later I felt the sensation again. When a flea is crawling on your skin, it creates a peculiar, tingling sensation.

"Something is definitely on me," I muttered.

Jumping out of bed, I went into the bathroom, closed the door, and flicked on the light.

At first, I didn't see anything. Then what I assumed was a freckle began to crawl. I touched it with a fingertip and it sprang off my leg and into the sink.

I wasn't familiar with fleas. We had never experienced fleas in Africa. And although I had lived in some deplorable hovels in college, they had never been flea infested.

Now I sat in the posh office of a French executive with one moving up my leg. I let out my breath in a quick gasp. Monsieur Fayolle gazed at me through slitted eyes, as if cigarette smoke was drifting into his face. He wasn't smoking.

"A problem?" he asked.

"No, no," I replied. "Now where were we?"

The flea crawled up the back of my leg, past my knee, and up to my thigh. Please, God, I thought. Don't let him crawl any higher.

"Is this the correct way to say it?" Monsieur Fayolle asked. "There is a lot of people in the bank today."

"Not quite," I replied, as the flea inched up my thigh one hop at a time, pausing to do whatever he was doing beneath my trousers—perhaps locating a tasty place to bite, and then moving on again. I wanted to scream.

"It's there *are*," I said.

"Oh, yes," Monsieur Fayolle said, nodding. "There are a lot of people in the bank today."

"Market," I said. He knew the drill.

"There are a lot of people in the market today."

"Very good," I said, sweat trickling down my cheeks. God, get me out of here!

When the lesson ended, I jumped up, shook Monsieur Fayolle's hand, and headed toward the door.

He stopped me about halfway across his office.

"I'm having a small dinner party at my house on Thursday evening," he said. "You are invited ... and your wife of course."

"Thank you," I said, gave a slight nod, and hurried into the hallway.

Fortunately, it was a large office building and had a bathroom on each floor. Racing into a stall, I dropped my pants, found the flea, and crushed it on the counter.

"Ahhh," I sighed.

Then I began to chuckle. This was the happiest moment of my day—*not* to have a flea crawling up my leg!

What a relief!

I was certainly leading the debonair Parisian life.

The following Thursday evening, Claudia and I attended Monsieur Fayolle's dinner party. It was a small dinner party indeed—we were the only guests. And it was an enlightening experience. This man was the assistant director of a large insurance company. I had expected the accommodations to be lavish, the food delicious. Instead, a generic white fish and pieces of fried potatoes that resembled tater-tots lined out plates. As his wife—who seemed more like a servant than a spouse—served us, I glanced at Monsieur Fayolle. He was watching us closely. This was a lesson, I realized. He was putting me in my place. To him, I was nothing more than a lowly teacher-nowhere near his station in life or class.

My pride rose up and I wanted to give this pompous little bastard the finger. Then a little rhyme entered my thoughts and made me smile.

"Fayolle-Asshole."

It was perfect. He certainly was one.

After dinner, Monsieur Fayolle invited us to sit on his sofa. He sat across from us in a comfortable chair and took out a bottle of whiskey.

"Eighteen-year-old single malt scotch whiskey," he explained with a smile. "Very expensive."

"My," Claudia said, impressed.

"*Oui*," he replied, with a feminine pout of his thin dark lips. "I have a drink each evening."

He took out a crystal glass and poured in an inch of whiskey. I foolishly expected him to hand the glass over to Claudia and then pour one for me. But he picked it up and leaned back in his chair. He gave a sigh of contentment and sipped it with obvious appreciation while watching us over the rim of his glass.

Another lesson; we didn't deserve the expensive scotch.

"Well," I said, standing up. It occurred to me that perhaps we weren't supposed to stand until the assistant director had risen first, as was the protocol for the English royal family. "It's late. We should be going."

"Yes," Claudia said. "Thank you for the dinner."

Monsieur Fayolle nodded and continued to sip his scotch as we headed to the door. His wife escorted us out.

Down on the street, Claudia gazed at me.

"You have to work with that guy twice a week?" she asked. "How can you bear it?"

"He was putting us in our place," I said.

"He's so rude!" she said. "I wanted to take that bottle of scotch and pour it over his head!"

"What about the food?" I asked.

"I've had better tater-tots at McDonalds," she huffed. "What a joke."

"I have a new name for him," I said and told her.

Claudia giggled. "That's him all right."

In contrast to Ruben Fayolle, I worked with another French business executive who was one of the nicest people I had ever met.

Jean Gouraud was a tall, rugged man from Brittany. He was friendly and open and usually smiling. He worked for a sporting goods company and lacked the pompous absurdity of Monsieur Fayolle. Over the weeks of teaching, we became friends and occasionally met for lunch at a café near his office. He told me about his children; he had an 18-year-old son named Laurent, and a 14-year-old daughter named Sophie.

"Laurent wants to major in history at college," Jean told me. "But I want him to take a law degree."

We talked about his children, and then about his experience as a paratrooper in the French Army. Jean had fought in the Algerian War. This was a brutal, messy, complicated affair–both a war for independence, and a civil war among those who wanted to remain a French colony. The French population had gradually turned against the conflict, leading to demonstrations in Paris for withdraw from Algeria. Eventually, the demonstrators got their wish.

In the spring of 1962, France signed a treaty with the Front de Libération Nationale (FLN) giving Algeria its independence. President Charles de Gaulle withdrew his troops, leaving behind many Algerians who had supported the French to be murdered. In addition, some former French military remained loyal to French Algeria and formed an organization called the OAS. Their goal was to assassinate de Gaulle, whom they considered a traitor. Frederick Forsyth wrote a classic novel about this conflict titled <u>The Day of the Jackal</u>.

Jean Gouraud was involved in this war as a young soldier, and told me about it as we sat at the café.

"You and Claudia must come for dinner," he said one afternoon. "I would like you to meet Yvette and the children."

The Gourauds lived in Chevillé, a beautiful hamlet nestled in the forêt de Chevillé. Claudia and I caught a train at the Gare St.-Lazare and Jean met us at the station. She had brought a potted plant as a gift for his wife.

"*Ah, vous-êtes très gentilé,*" Yvette exclaimed when Claudia gave her the plant. "*Merci.*"

Yvette was a lovely woman with a clear, healthy face, sparkling eyes, and a charming smile. We met Laurent and Sophie, who were both eager, curious teenagers. I thought Jean would have a loving family and I was right. He was a good man and had helped to foster a loving home life.

We sat down to dinner and Yvette served peppered roast beef with potatoes *Dauphinois*, balsamic mushrooms, and honey Dijon Brussels sprouts. Jean filled our wine glasses with a very smooth Cabernet Sauvignon. We had a lively conversation and Laurent and Sophie wanted to know everything about life in the states. They mentioned several movie stars and asked if we knew them personally. Sophie wanted to know if we had visited the White House. How many horses did we own? Was it true that all Americans talked like they did in the movies? Laurent told us he really liked war movies.

"I'm sure your father has told you stories about his war experiences in Algeria," I said.

Laurent looked confused. "What?"

Jean spoke up immediately. "I think perhaps you have me mixed up with another student," he said. "I was never in Algeria."

His hazel eyes flickered imploringly over mine and I got the message.

"Oh, yeah," I said. "I'm getting you mixed up with Monsieur Fayolle."

"Jean was never in Algeria," Yvette spoke up. "That horrible war. So brutal … so tragic!"

"Yvette was a protestor against the war," Jean explained. "At the university."

"Ah," I muttered. Now I understood.

"It's better to die standing than to live on your knees," she continued with surprising bitterness. "The Algerians believed this."

"It would take a lot of courage," Claudia said.

"Oh, yes," Yvette said, her bright smile returning.

I felt we had dodged a very large bullet-more like a cannonball or surface-to-air missile.

"How about rock stars?" Sophie asked. "Do you know any of them?"

We laughed and everyone became merry again.

"Time for dessert," Yvette said.

She stepped into the kitchen and returned with plates of crème caramel. Jean poured glasses of champagne.

When I finished my champagne, he filled my glass again. This was turning out to be a wonderful evening. I felt the Cabernet Sauvignon and champagne flowing through me. Then I thought about Fayolle and our appalling dinner with him. He had put us in our place, all right. Jean and his family, on the other hand, treated us like valued guests.

After dinner, we settled on comfortable chairs in the living room and Jean produced a bottle of Rémy Martin cognac.

"Very good," he said, pouring it carefully into a glass.

I glanced at Claudia. She knew what I was thinking and lifted her dark eyebrows. Now was the time for us to be put in our place.

It didn't happen.

"Here," Jean said, handing Claudia the glass.

Yvette laughed. "Jean loves to play the bartender."

He gave me a glass and then his wife. When we all had a drink in our hands, he raised his in toast.

"To friends," Jean said. "*Bon santé.*"

"*Bon santé*," we all repeated.

On the return to the Chevillé train station, Jean drove us through the forest. It took a few minutes longer, but he wanted to talk.

"I am sorry," he began, "but Yvette knows nothing about my involvement in the Algerian War."

"You've never told her?" Claudia asked, astonished.

"Never," he said. "She would not understand. And it would change her impression of me. I could not endure this."

"Wow," I exclaimed. "Sorry I mentioned it."

"No, No," Jean said. "It was my fault. I should have warned you not to say anything about the war in front of my family."

"You think it's okay now?" Claudia asked.

"Oh, yes," Jean said. "Yvette thinks it was simply a misunderstanding."

"In a way, it was," I commented.

"Yes," he said, grinning. "*Ç'est vrai.*"

On the train, Claudia fell asleep with her head nestled against my shoulder. It was nearly midnight and I could see nothing of the passing fields and towns, only the dim green glow of the interior coach lights reflecting off the glass. I shook my head, thinking about the two very different dinner experiences we'd had with French businessmen.

Fayolle had treated us as inferiors. Gouraud had treated us like friends. Wasn't this the way it always was with people you met? Some thought you were wonderful, and some thought you were excrement on the sole of their shoe. In the long run, it didn't matter. Trying to find your value through others was for suckers, although I'd found that life *was* easier when people liked you. It depended on what you had to trade for their approval.

I thought about Jean and how he had to hide his war experience from his wife. It must have been difficult to never talk about what he'd seen in Algeria or how the war had affected him. He didn't appear to be suffering from PTSD, but if he were, he would have had to deal with it alone.

The train gave a lurch as we rounded a curve, and I grinned. No matter what I thought about our treatment, I was, after all, the teacher with a flea crawling up his leg during a lesson.

This put things into perspective.

Chapter 10
The Paris Free Voice

The sky was like a white marble dome as I walked down the Avenue Winston Churchill toward the river. When I reached the Cours de la Reine, I veered right to the Pont des Invalides. The trees along the Seine had turned yellow, gold, and brown. The current was fast and the water muddy from the rains.

I was headed to the offices of the Paris Free Voice Newspaper, located in the basement of the American Church. The editor, Rob Parsons, greeted me with a shy nod. He was an interesting character – quietly introverted at times, interspersed with moments of extreme cheerfulness and laughter. I never knew which Rob I would meet, so I entered his office hesitantly. He must have felt the same way about me, because our conversations were usually friendly but tentative, like two friends preparing to compete and not knowing which one was best.

Three of his staff writers sat at desks in the office. Julie was an Italian/American who wrote the jazz notes section of the paper. She also worked as a rock music promoter and had recently gone to dinner with Stevie Wonder. Abby was English and wrote feature stories on women's issues. Slumped on a chair in the corner with his feet up on a desk was Neal, an Irishman from Galway who covered sporting events around Paris – especially the horse races.

The Paris Free Voice wasn't a hard-news paper like the International Herald Tribune, but a local tabloid for Americans living in Paris.

"Got something for you," Rob said as I stepped into his office.

"Great," I said. I hadn't written anything for him yet and was eager to get started. Perhaps it wasn't Le Monde, but I wanted to see my byline appear on a Paris publication.

"There's going to be an anti-Israel demonstration on the Place de Republique tomorrow," he said. "Will you cover it?"

"Sure," I said.

I'd seen demonstrations in Paris before. The city was a mirror held up to the world. Whatever was happening politically–even in remote sections of the globe–reflected on the French streets in protests or demonstrations. With its gray woolen sky, old buildings, and traffic passing on damp pavements, Paris became the backdrop for whatever reality the world chose.

"I'll send David with you."

David Levy was the staff photographer.

We met the next afternoon at a café on the rue du Temple and walked up to the Place de Republique. About a thousand people were marching and carrying anti-Israel signs. They had gathered on the eastern edge of the Place and were now moving up the avenue shouting, "NO ANNEXATION!"

We followed them for a few minutes and David snapped photos.

I was chatting about how people in Paris had a fifth gear–a fast gear–and after two languid years in Africa I wasn't used to it, when I glanced over and saw David was sweating. He looked nervous. I began to ask what was troubling him, when I realized the situation. He was afraid the demonstrators would notice a young Jewish photographer following on the sidewalk and snapping photos. They didn't seem dangerous at the moment, but I had seen things get out of hand with crowds in Kinshasa. The escalation could spark quickly.

"Have you got the shots you need?" I asked.

"Yeah," he replied, keeping his eyes on the crowd.

"Okay then," I said. "I'll meet you back at the office."

"You sure?" he asked.

"Yeah. I'll stick around and do a few interviews."

David nodded with relief and slipped away into the watchers on the sidewalk. I admired his courage. My heritage was Scottish, Irish,

English, and German. I had one of those generic European faces that made people think I was from a variety of countries. I'd even gotten into a dispute with a Belgian hotel clerk once when I handed her my passport.

"This is an *American* passport," she had said, her eyes narrowing.

"That's right," I replied, thinking about how I was going to catch a train the next morning.

"But you *aren't* American," she said.

I stopped thinking about the train.

"What?" I asked.

"You are Canadian," she said.

"No, really," I said. "I'm American."

She stood back from the counter and folded her arms.

"You speak French with a Canadian accent ... you look Canadian ... and yet you give me an *American* passport. What are you trying to do, hum?"

I thought for a moment, stunned by the ridiculousness of the situation.

At last, I said, "My grandfather was Canadian."

"*Ah bon*," she huffed. "Your grandfather. You see, I can always spot these things."

She accepted my passport now and I gave a sigh of relief as I climbed the hotel stairs to my room.

That was a hilarious mix-up. But at no time in Europe had I ever felt in danger because of the way I looked. We took precautions about being in certain areas of Paris at night as you would any large city. But during the day, we felt safe.

The following Wednesday, the newspaper came out with my feature and David's photographs on the front page. I was delighted to see a man reading it on the Métro, and even more so when our school director passed out copies at a staff meeting.

"Well done, Hemingway," Jack said. "When are you going to publish your first novel?"

To celebrate, Claudia suggested we go out for dinner. A friend had told us about the restaurant Beaux Arts off the Boulevard Saint Germaine. The place was old and smoky; the area filled with nightlife. The hotel where Oscar Wilde had died was nearby and the famous café Deux Magots.

Afterwards, we had a drink at the Café Napoleon. On the street corner, a man was entertaining people with trained rats. Tilting his head back, he put a gray rat into his mouth so that only the pink tail protruded from between his lips.

Claudia put a hand to her mouth and turned away. The man quickly pulled out the squirming rat and grinned.

"*Oui, Madame,*" he said. "It is disgusting. But you watch *n'est-ce pas?* You watch!"

"I'd be more worried if I was the rat," I said. "Who knows where his mouth has been?"

Claudia laughed.

On afternoons when I wasn't teaching, I would often drop by the Paris Free Voice to see what was happening.

Sometimes Rob would say, "Thirsty?" and we would go to a café for a beer and talk about the scramble to make deadlines, the problems of working with a transient staff, how to increase distribution, and the constant financial strain to keep the paper running.

One day in December, he jumped up from his desk when I entered the office.

"Christmas gifts!" he yelled.

This was the out-going Rob, the boisterous, loud-talking, cheerful guy. I was immediately on my guard.

"What?" I asked, confused.

"Gifts with a French accent," he said. "What do people buy for their friends back home?"

I thought about it for a moment and nodded. "Could make an interesting seasonal feature."

"Great," he said. "It's yours."

"But ..." I stammered. "I don't know anything about that."

"So what?" he said, clapping me on the back. "You research it, write it, and get it back to me by Monday. The details don't make any difference."

This assignment wasn't within my area of expertise or comfort, but I knew someone who could help.

"French Christmas gifts?" Claudia asked.

"For friends back home," I stressed.

She thought for a moment. "What would you get *your* friends? Let's start there."

"I don't know," I said, baffled. "An old poster from a stand along the river, a miniature Eiffel Tower. It depends on the recipient. If it's one of your brothers, I'd get him a pack of those funny condoms they sell on the rue St.-Denis."

Claudia looked horrified. "No, no, no," she said, holding a hand to her forehead. "These have to be *quality* gifts."

"That's why I need your help," I said.

For the next few days, we went from store to store, investigating possible gifts and their prices. We looked at jewelry, perfume, scarves, wine, chocolates, canned duck, cheese, ties for men, pocket knives, wine openers, and dozens of other items that might make enjoyable gifts back home and were easily mailed or shipped.

In the end, I had enough to write the feature and get it to Rob on deadline. When the story was printed, however, I had no sense of accomplishment. It was simply an assignment I had completed.

Standing there with the newspaper in my hand, I thought back to the man with the rats. Wasn't my article on French Christmas gifts similar in entertainment value to a guy who swallowed rats on the Boulevard St.-Germain? I felt like it was, and this diminished my excitement.

"Yes, the story is silly crap," I wanted to say. "But you read it, *n'est-ce pas?* You read it!"

***

Follow-up:
David had reason to be nervous at the anti-Israel demonstration. Anti-Semitic tensions ran high in those days. One of our favorite places to eat lunch was Goldenberg's Deli on the rue des Rosiers in the Marais quarter. The food was delicious and we enjoyed the cheerful atmosphere. A red border stating JO GOLDENBERG with a Star of David on either side ran across the front of the deli. The border was trimmed in yellow. Scrumptious pastries decorated the large front window.

The deli was colorful, quaint, and a wonderful place to meet with friends. It shocked us when two men (members of the Abu Nidal Organization) attacked the deli on August 9 of that year. After tossing a grenade among the seated customers, they opened fire with machine guns. Six people were killed, including two Americans, and twenty-two people wounded. BusinessWeek called it 'the heaviest toll suffered on Jews in France since WWII.'

ברך אותם הו אדון

Chapter 11
The Poet's Corner

The light in the Jardin des Tuileries was an artist's light—bright and clear, although Monet could have painted wonderful scenes with the gray light that had filtered over Paris during the past few weeks. I was happy to be outside after several days of drenching rain and turned up the gravel path toward the rue de Rivoli.

When I reached the English bookstore W. H. Smith, I stepped inside. I was looking for a book on the life of George Adamson, a game warden in Kenya known for his work with the lions of Kitengela. My wife and I had moved to Paris from Africa, and the memory of our life there was like a spell that had entered my blood and mingled with my spirit, causing me to dream of the dry savannah.

To my delight, they had the book. I paid for it and was heading toward the door when I spied a familiar face. Shauna Mulloy was a young poet we had met at one of Hailey Barrow's parties. She was slender, with short brown hair and wire-rimmed glasses. She usually dressed in dark clothes: black turtle-neck sweaters, dark jeans, long charcoal-gray coats, and black boots.

"It's been a while," she said.

It had been a while, and for a reason.

A few months before, Shauna had borrowed my new hardback copy of *Hunger* by Knut Hamsun. I had recently purchased it at Shakespeare & Company. When she returned it weeks later, the book appeared as if a car had run over it. Could Shauna have possibly left it in the street? I was not pleased.

"How's the poetry going?" I asked.

"I'm giving a reading at the Centre Pompidou," she replied. "Sponsored by the Canadian Cultural Center."

"That's quite a compliment," I said.

"Yes," she said. "But I'm worried about John."

89

John Craig was Shauna's boyfriend. They shared an apartment. He also wanted to be a poet and was highly competitive.

"He's jealous I was invited and he wasn't," she explained.

"He's a good guy," I said. "I'm sure he'll be happy for you."

"You think so?" she asked.

I didn't know if this was true or not, but what could I say?

Shauna smiled. "I'm giving a party on Wednesday evening. Nothing big ... just sitting around and sipping wine. You and Claudia should come."

"I'll ask her," I said.

My wife considered the invitation thoughtfully. "Is she going to read her poetry?"

Claudia wasn't a big fan of Shauna's work. Her favorite poet was Emily Dickinson.

"She didn't mention it," I replied. "Said we'd be sipping wine."

"Isn't that like the perfect time for a poet to share her work?"

"Guess so," I said.

Shauna's apartment was near the Bastille. We arrived at nine o'clock, expecting to hear soothing guitar music and to see the flicker of candles. Instead, we were shocked to find the place jammed with people. It was nothing like the cozy evening she had described.

"Still wanna go in?" I asked.

"Who knows?" Claudia said, gazing at the crowd. "Might be fun."

Shauna had invited a variety of guests. We were introduced to Miguel, an 18-year-old boy who played beautiful Spanish guitar music, a clothes designer with his hair slicked back with what must have been a whole can of grease, several writers and poets, a songwriter who said he wrote all his music while walking around Paris, ("I prefer to get out on the streets and hum the music and think of the lyrics instead of sitting home at my piano," he explained.) and a jazz saxophone player from New York City who talked in a low, smooth, late-night smoky voice.

Eventually, I found myself beside a woman from Mississippi who wrote for travel magazines. Vivian was small and thin with graying blonde hair. With her southern accent, she pronounced the word *store* as 'stowah'.

"We went to that *stowah*," she said, referring to the Galleries Lafayette.

I don't remember what she'd been looking for, but whatever it was, she hadn't found it.

"You wanted *mowah* from the *stowah*?" I asked, feeling witty.

Vivian shot me a glance. Apparently, she didn't find my humor amusing. Oh, well. I'd already chugged several beers. Or was that *beeahs*?

"I met William Faulkner, you know," she said.

"That must've been exciting," I replied. Faulkner was one of my favorite writers.

"It was," she said and refilled her wineglass.

"When did you meet him?"

"Oh, just a few years ago … when I was at the university."

I considered this for a moment. Vivian looked to be about sixty years old.

"Faulkner has been dead since 1961," I remarked.

"Has it been that long?" she mused and looked surprised.

"What was he like?" I asked.

"A little man with a large head and bushy gray hair," she replied. "And bless his heart, he had a strong southern accent."

"Like you," I said.

Vivian smiled. "Why *yayes*."

Next, I bumped into a young woman with a great crop of frizzy brown hair. She was an illustrator who had submitted her drawings to several newspapers and magazines.

"Do I look crazy to you?" she asked.

I gazed at her. She was small and perky, with large wondrous eyes.

"I only ask," she continued, because John thinks I'm crazy."

"John Craig?"

"Yeh. He lives with my sister."

"Oh, then you're ..."

"Cara Mulloy." She held out a hand.

"Nice to meet you," I said.

Cara made a little dance move, though the music had stopped playing.

"I was a real terror as a child," she said, tapping a black fingernail against her chin. "Going around the neighborhood in December and breaking every Christmas light I could get my hands on just to hear them pop!"

"Well ... I ..."

"POP!" she cried.

Shauna came over to us. She was wearing a black fedora, gray jacket, white shirt with a red bow tie, black slacks, and red boots. She looked like a cross between a gangster and a Broadway dancer.

"Cara and her Christmas lights," she said and laughed.

"POP!" Cara cried again.

Shauna took me by the arm. "I want you to meet someone."

I waved goodbye to Cara, who was still dancing to her own music. She held up a hand and moved the tips of her fingers in a bye-bye gesture, showing her black fingernails.

Shauna and I crossed the room to a young man and woman standing near the wine table.

The young man's name was Morgan and the young woman was his French wife, Celeste. He wore a tailored suit and tie. She wore a pale-blue and silver gown that looked like it might have once belonged to Audrey Hepburn. I was sure I'd seen it in one of her ritzy movies. Celeste topped this off with a diamond necklace. I imagined the young couple had just come from the opera or some other place where wealthy people spent their evenings.

"Morgan wants to be a writer, but doesn't know much about the business," Shauna said. "I thought maybe you could advise him."

Morgan flashed me a bright grin and held out his hand. Even his grin looked expensive.

"He went to Princeton," Shauna added and left me standing there with the two of them gazing at me.

"What kind of books do you write?" I asked.

If Morgan had told me he was in the middle of writing *This Side of Paradise*, I would have believed him.

"Philosophy," he said.

I relaxed. This wasn't Scott Fitzgerald; this was Kierkegaard.

"I don't know much about that kind of work," I said. "Have you finished the book?"

Celeste squeezed her husband's arm. "He is about halfway through," she said. "*N'est-ce pas vrai, Chérie?*"

Morgan blushed. "It's taking a while."

"Keep at it," I said.

"That's why we're here," he said. "We're roughing it in Paris until I get the book done."

I glanced at Celeste to see if she appreciated the irony. Apparently, she didn't. She was nodding in total agreement.

"*There* you are," Claudia said.

I introduced her to Morgan and Celeste.

"Just visiting?" Claudia asked.

"No," Celeste replied. "We live here."

Claudia smiled and discreetly scanned Celeste from head to toe. "Wonderful."

"Roughing it," Morgan added.

"Aren't we all," I said.

The four of us were quiet for a moment.

"We should be going," Claudia suggested.

I glanced at my watch. It was nearly two o'clock and I had classes in the morning.

Morgan looked at his wife and then turned to us.

"We're leaving too," he said. "Can we give you a lift?"

The Métro was closed and it was sprinkling outside. Anyway, how often did one have a chance to play a character in *The Great Gatsby?*

"Thank you," Claudia responded. "I just got these shoes. I don't want to get them wet."

Celeste looked at the shoes and smiled.

We made a round of the room and said our goodbyes. Cara was sitting in Miguel's lap while he strummed his guitar. Vivian was pouring herself another glass of wine and probably telling someone she had met Harper Lee. The songwriter was beating out a tune on the leg of his jeans. Shauna and John were tucked away in a corner, holding a serious conversation. I didn't want to interrupt them, but we didn't want to be rude.

When we got down to the street, Celeste took out her car keys. Lifting the edge of her fur coat, she hurried through the drizzle to a sleek new Mercedes.

"My car," she said.

"She needed something to get around Paris while I'm writing," Morgan explained.

"Well, sure," I said.

They dropped us off at our apartment on the rue de Malte. It had stopped raining, so we lingered on the curb and waved as they drove away.

Claudia frowned.

"What's the matter?" I asked.

"He's roughing it in Paris and his wife is wearing a fur coat and diamond earrings!"

"Reminds me of us," I said.

She laughed. "Think we'll ever see them again?"

"Not a chance. And if we did, we probably couldn't afford it."

She put her arms around my shoulders. "Know what our problem is?"

"What?"

"We're reverse snobs," she said. "We don't like them because they have money."

"Maybe they don't," I suggested. "Maybe her coat and diamonds are fake, and they rented the car."

Claudia grinned delightedly. "What a wonderful thought."

Our street and apartment building no longer seemed so shabby. In fact, it was a wonderful place to live, and we were happy to be there. Even if we did have to fumigate the rooms for fleas, tape old French posters over the red bordello wallpaper, and put a wine cork under one of the table legs.

"Morgan and Celeste might have a better address," I said. "But they don't have a better life."

"So true," Claudia said and we hurried upstairs.

Two days later it was raining again when I came out of the Métro near the rue St. Maur. A large beech tree near the station glowed red and green in the traffic lights. The store fronts and apartment buildings were streaked dark and looked somber. The rain intensified as I walked, so I pulled out my umbrella. On the cobblestones behind the old St. Joseph Church, a flock of pigeons pecked at soggy bread crumbs.

When I reached our apartment, Claudia was curled up on the couch with a blanket over her legs. She looked warm and comfortable and I realized that even in Paris one could only be busy so many days and then you needed to take a break. This was especially true in the wet weather, when you felt the need to stay inside against the dampness that pervaded the city. On these days you wore heavy sweaters and drank lots of hot tea or coffee, ate bowls of hearty soup, and appreciated the warmth of your kitchen stove.

"John called," she said, putting down the book she was reading. "He wants to meet you at six."

"Where?"

"The Café des Arts."

"You wanna come?" I asked.

Claudia pulled the blanket around her. "Are we still going out to dinner?"

"I was planning on it."

"Good," she said. "I'll meet you at the restaurant."

John and I had only spoken briefly at Shauna's party, mainly because he was miffed about her being asked to read her poetry at the Centre Pompidou.

And there was something else.

Recently, John and Shauna had formed a writing group that met every Wednesday. I had gone the week before for the first time and found it interesting, though not directly helpful. John wanted acclaim for his poetry. On this occasion, however, he had written a short story and asked me to read it. When I made a few suggestions to improve the story, he sat upright in his chair and gazed at me.

"You're a shitty poet," he snapped.

I stopped talking and looked at him. I wasn't interested in writing poetry and John knew this. So where had the sudden antagonism come from?

"Oh, God," Shauna sighed, removing her glasses and massaging the space between her eyebrows with a thumb and two fingertips.

"You don't want me to continue?" I asked.

"No," he snapped again. "I don't!"

"Okay," I said and tossed his typed pages onto the coffee table. I glanced at my watch. "Guess I'll be going. Thanks Shauna."

Some writers couldn't take criticism. Journalism taught me that writing was a craft like being a carpenter and all sincere comments helped the work. If a reader didn't like something I'd written, I wasn't offended. I wanted to know why they thought what they did. If I considered their opinion valid, (I only showed my work to readers I trusted or respected) I would work on it. My motto was: *You won't hurt my feelings by telling me what you think. That's how I make the writing better. If you don't tell me what you truly believe, you aren't helping.*

I'd gone to journalism school all dewy-eyed with a romantic vision of writing. I pictured myself sitting at a café with a special pen and paper and the morning light filtering through the maple trees. Only in this way would I achieve my best writing–or so I thought. My journalism professor had quickly knocked this idealism out of my head.

"This is bullshit," he said, crumpling up a feature I'd written and tossing it into the trash. "Do it over again and have it in by five o'clock or don't come back!"

Writing was a craft; you kept doing it until you got it right. Of course, there were different levels of ability, but that was a question of innate talent.

Therefore, John's harsh reaction to my feedback surprised me.

It was fitting that he wanted to meet at the Café des Arts on the Place de la Contrescarpe. The square with its tall white buildings, damp cobblestones, and small park set off by black posts and chains was near the apartment where the French poet Paul Verlaine had died. The area also was famous because Ernest Hemingway had lived around the corner on the rue du Cardinal Lemoine.

I took a seat beneath the café awning. The plastic sheeting was up and the heater was blasting hot air. I watched shoppers going in and out of a Charcuterie across the street. I was gazing at this timeless scene when I heard John's voice.

"Greetings," he said.

He had been eating a spinach crepe as he came up the street and had spilled it all over his jeans.

I handed him a napkin.

"Have you ordered yet?" he asked.

"Just got here."

John tossed the last of his crepe into a nearby trashcan.

"I was thinking we could go to a café down the street," he offered. "This place is too touristy."

"Fine," I said and followed him along the rue Descartes until we cut left past the Lycée Henri IV and down a quaint stretch to the rue l'École Polytechnique.

The Bar de l'X was on the corner. I had never been to this bar and gazed around curiously as we entered. A marble-topped bar and wooden tables and chairs and filled the warm interior. Fortunately, it didn't contain any of the obnoxious pin-ball or electronic games that were springing up in cafés all over Paris. The place felt comfortable and unassuming.

We took a seat by the window.

"Nice bar," I commented. "No machines."

John grinned. "I like it because of the girls."

I glanced at the tables around us. Young women with long hair, short skirts, dark stockings, and boots sipped wine and talked quietly. Many wore Algerian scarves, which were popular at the time.

"Students?" I asked.

"From the Sorbonne," he said and lifted his eyebrows.

The waiter came over and we ordered two beers.

"I wanted to talk with you about Shauna," he said.

"Problems?" I asked.

John frowned. "We're almost too much alike to make it work."

He and Shauna were both introspective, serious, and determined to be poets. I knew how everyone said opposites attracted, but I thought for a lasting relationship, the more you had in common with your partner, the better. You wanted to be with someone who understood what you were talking about. It was much better to have them say, "Sure, I get it. I feel the same way."

Now here was John the poet saying he and his girlfriend were too much alike. And he was saying this while ogling a bunch of university girls.

"Then get out of it," I suggested.

"Not so easy," he said. "We live together."

"Who lived there first?"

John thought for a moment. "We kinda found it together. Neither of us could afford the rent alone."

"Then you have to decide how badly you want out," I said. "Enough to lose the apartment?"

He laughed. "No."

I motioned to the waiter for two more beers.

"Well then," I said. "You either stay with Shauna and try to make it work, or get her to move out."

"You think she would?" he asked.

"How should I know?" I replied. "She's your girlfriend. Only you know the depth of your relationship. Maybe she'd be happy if you broke up."

John grinned. "Her sister's kinda hot. Did you see Cara at the party?"

"Likes to pop Christmas lights," I said.

"Right," he said and chuckled.

"So, you'd rather be with her?"

"Sure," he said.

"Then break up with Shauna and go after her sister. Older sisters always love that."

"You're kidding, right?" John asked.

"Right."

He grinned. "Actually, I would, except …"

"What?"

"Shauna has so many poetry contacts. I'd have to start all over again in Paris if I broke up with her."

"Are you going to her reading at the Centre?"

"Guess so," he replied. "Never know who you'll meet."

I glanced at my watch. "Gotta go. I'm meeting Claudia for dinner."

"Where?" he asked.

"The Restaurant Beaux Arts."

"Nice place."

"Good luck with the writing," I said.

John looked at me. "You're still a shitty poet."

"And your fiction sucks," I said.

John laughed. "Wanna get together for a drink next Wednesday before the meeting?"

"Okay," I said, knowing I might have a beer, but wouldn't go to the meeting. Nor would I read his prose.

Outside, the damp wind tugged at my jacket as I turned toward the Boulevard St.-Michel. When I reached the Boulevard St. Germain, I turned left and headed up to the Restaurant Beaux Arts. Claudia was standing outside the restaurant, reading the menu. She wore a dark gray wool coat and a thick scarf. She looked snuggly warm.

"How'd it go?" she asked.

"He wants to break up with Shauna, but doesn't wanna lose her poetry contacts."

"That guy," she said.

We entered the restaurant. A hostess led us to a table.

"There's more," I said.

"What?"

"He wants to go out with Cara."

"Her sister?" Claudia laughed. "He's delusional."

"They might make a good match."
"Oh, stop," she said.

Chapter 12
The Three-Dinner Weekend

Looking out the rain-streaked taxi window at 2am as we sped along the Seine, I saw the Eiffel Tower looming vast and gray across the water, the Place de la Concorde with its myriad of round street lamps resembling fire flies hovering above a frosted-field, the arched entrance and high walls of the Louvre, the brightly lit Tour Saint Jacques at Chatelet, and then we were speeding up the Boulevard de Sebastopol toward home.

We were returning from a dinner with the ABC TV Correspondent Greg Dobbs. Greg had transferred to Paris from London a month before. Now he lived in an elegant apartment on the Place d'Alma. The apartment was on the *quatrième étage* (fifth floor) and had large windows that overlooked the Seine, the Quay D'Orsay, and the Eiffel Tower. As we sat at the dinner table, the room was softly lit with lights from passing boats, their deck lights twinkling in colorful strands for dining. Greg's Emmy Award for Journalism glinted on the mantle. He received it for his coverage of the recent Italian earthquake.

"*Merci et bon appetite,*" he said, lifting a wine glass.

Greg was small, wiry, and energetic, with dark hair graying at the temples. His hawk eyes glowed with concentrated intelligence.

Claudia was seated on my right and chatting happily with Greg's wife, Carol, whom she had known since college.

On my left sat a young man named Edward, who had worked for Greg in London. Beyond him was a tall, slender, tough-looking woman in a green leather jump suit. This was Greg's TV producer. Across the table sat her French husband and a young woman from Minneapolis who seemed very nice and had also recently moved to Paris from London.

103

For dinner, they served us broccoli soup, lamb with Spanish-style beans, Camembert cheese, pears in sangria, and white wine.

"That's really something," I said to Greg, motioning to the golden-winged woman holding up a sphere on his mantle.

He grinned. "It goes to the entire team. Not just me."

His modesty impressed me, considering his position.

"And you've just returned from Warsaw?"

He nodded. I'd been told he took eighteen boxes of supplies with him to hand out.

Edward leaned over to me.

"My father wrote So&So's latest book," he whispered, mentioning the name of a famous journalist.

"You're kidding," I said.

"Not at all," he replied. "The journalist is too busy to write his own books, and my father is nobody … so he writes the books and So&So publishes them under his name."

"Your father is okay with that?" I asked.

"Oh, yes," Edward said. "He gets paid for the writing and the journalist promotes the books. Everyone is happy."

After dinner, Greg's producer mentioned press objectivity and we got into a heated discussion. Everyone thought their point of view was the correct one.

I glanced at Greg and saw him smiling.

Later, when we were downstairs and waiting for a taxi, Claudia gazed up at the ornate apartment building. "I could never live like that," she said. "Could you?"

"Sure," I replied. "I could live in their apartment easily."

"I'm surprised," she said.

"Why? It's beautiful. And what a view!"

"Still …" she muttered.

"I don't think we have to worry about it. Maybe someday …"

"Good," she said with a huff.

"What's wrong? You afraid we'll be corrupted?"

"I've seen it happen," she said. Her parents moved in a circle of wealthy friends and acquaintances.

"Don't you think people who've been corrupted by wealth would've been corrupted by something else if they were poor?" I asked.

Claudia laughed. "Never thought about it like that."

"Anyway," I continued. "Greg and Carol are wonderful."

"They are," she said.

We slept late the next morning and when I stumbled into the kitchen Claudia shouted, "Don't eat anything!"

She was combing her hair in the bathroom.

"Why?" I called.

"We have the Vietnamese luncheon today. It's already after ten."

Claudia had become friends with an older Vietnamese couple at the International Refugee School. They had invited us for lunch.

"Is this going to be a big deal?" I asked, not in the mood for another social event.

"No, no," she replied. "They just want to have us over."

"Okay," I said. "I'll run across the street and pick up a bottle of wine."

"And flowers," she added.

"And flowers," I called and hurried down the stairs.

An hour later, we were on the Métro and headed toward the Avenue de Clichy. I had cheated and gotten a croissant at the boulangerie, which I hastily stuffed down as I headed to the wine shop. Otherwise, I hadn't eaten anything and I was already getting hungry.

We knocked on the Nguyen's apartment door and stood back.

"Remember," I said. "We can't stay long. We have that dinner at the Chateau this evening."

"That's tonight?"

"Yes."

"Well," she said. "It's only lunchtime."

An elderly gentleman in black silk clothes greeted us. He waved us inside, smiling, and speaking in Vietnamese, which unfortunately, neither of us understood. His wife came from another room and clapped her hands joyfully.

"Oh," she sighed. "We are happy you have come. Please ..."

She escorted us down the hallway to a large living room. To my surprise, half a dozen elderly people in traditional Vietnamese clothes sat in chairs around the room. In the corner were two younger people dressed in typical French clothes. Mrs. Nguyen introduced us to her father and mother, her brother and his wife, her uncle, her son and his girlfriend, and a gentleman named Mr. Tran. I wasn't sure if Mr. Tran was family or a friend.

They all greeted us warmly as Mrs. Nguyen told them about Claudia and her work as a teacher at the refugee school. This wasn't simply a lunch. These people were all here to pay respect to my wife, and it was obvious they took the event seriously. I was ashamed because we hadn't understood their intentions; hadn't given the luncheon the respect it deserved. I was wearing blue jeans and scruffy brown shoes. It was October, so I was wearing a button-down shirt with a navy-blue sweater and that helped, but still ...

Claudia was also wearing jeans. She glanced at me and I saw the embarrassment in her eyes.

"I never expected ..." she whispered and let it trail off.

Mrs. Nguyen guided us to a large wooden table in the dining room.

I love Vietnamese cooking and my stomach rumbled at the delicious smells emanating from the kitchen. Mrs. Nguyen brought out a large ceramic bowl of noodle soup.

"*Pho,*" she said, pointing to the soup. "*Pho.*"

She ladled the soup out to us. It consisted of broth, fresh rice noodles, herbs, and slices of chicken. I took a spoonful and it was delicious. As I was hungry, I quickly finished my bowl and Mrs. Nguyen filled it up again with another ladle.

After the second bowl, I leaned back contented.

"It's so good," Claudia said to our host.

"Thank my mother," Mrs. Nguyen replied, and motioned to the elderly woman seated at the far end of the table. "She make it."

The old lady nodded shyly.

Mrs. Nguyen's sister-in-law entered the dining room carrying a tray of spring rolls.

I might have room for one, I told myself. I was getting full, but I loved the fresh flavor of spring rolls made from salad greens, coriander, and cooked shrimp wrapped in transparent pancakes. They came with a small bowl of fish sauce for dipping.

I quickly ate one and Mrs. Nguyen gave me another.

"Maybe just one more," I whispered to Claudia.

I had barely finished the second spring roll when a clay pot was placed in the center of the table. Inside the pot were hunks of fish in caramelized brown sauce. Mrs. Nguyen spooned rice onto our plates and served portions of the fish and sauce onto the rice.

Oh, Lord, it was fantastic-spicy and sweet. But where was I going to put it? My belt was already feeling tight. What a fool I'd been to eat a croissant before coming, and then to stuff myself on noodle soup and spring rolls.

Edging down my belt to give my stomach a bit more room, I finished my portion of the caramelized fish. But I had learned my lesson and politely declined another serving.

"You no like?" Mrs. Nguyen asked, her eyes looking sad.

"It's wonderful," I blurted. "But I'm getting a bit full."

She looked at me, feigning disappointment, and put down the ladle. Then she nodded to her sister-in-law, who went into the kitchen and returned once again with a large white platter.

"Vietnamese baked snapper," Mrs. Nguyen explained. "Very good."

A whole baked fish sprinkled with chopped lemongrass, mint leaves, basil leaves, coriander, and chopped roasted peanuts lay on the platter. It looked and smelled fantastic. Oh, why hadn't they brought this out first? I was stuffed to the point of discomfort, but I couldn't pass this up.

Claudia held a napkin to her mouth and whispered, "I can't eat another bite."

"I know," I replied, also in a whisper. "But it's so good."

"It's the best dinner I've ever had."

We devoured the snapper, and I leaned back in my chair triumphantly. The feeling of accomplishment, however, only lasted a moment.

"Baked white fish with lemon grass," Mrs. Nguyen announced, setting another platter on the table. "Very juicy."

The dinner continued in this way for several more entrees, ending in one of my favorite dishes in the world: soft-shell crabs. These were fried to a light golden crispiness and served on a bed of mint leaves and greens with hoisin dipping sauce sprinkled with chopped peanuts.

By now I felt sick and only managed two bites of the most succulent, delicious soft-shell crab I'd ever tasted. What a travesty. What an incredible disappointment.

For dessert, Mrs. Nguyen served deep-fried donut balls sprinkled with sesame seeds and filled with sweet bean paste. I could only look at them and shake my head. There wasn't room for one more ounce of food.

We finished lunch at around four o'clock and then sat talking and sipping tea for another hour. By the time we said our farewells and staggered out to the street, it was nearly five o'clock.

"We just have time to catch the train," Claudia said.

"You're kidding," I groaned.

***

Three young French entrepreneurs at our school had birthdays in October, so they had combined to throw one lavish party at a chateau in the country. To get there, we had to take the RER to Versailles and then walk half a mile up a narrow lane.

It was after dark when we entered the gate. The chateau's large windows were beautifully lit in soft yellow. A white gravel path led up to the main entrance. Ruben—one of the three birthday boys—greeted us at the door. He escorted us through the house to a broad lawn decorated with party lights. The lawn was crowded with people talking and laughing. Drink tables displayed chilled bottles of champagne, wine, and beer. Two large fires blazed on either side of the walk. A roast pig turned slowly on a spit above one of the fires. On the other was a roast lamb.

Pierre, the second birthday boy, came up to us with glasses of champagne.

"For you," he said merrily, handing us each a glass.

Claudia gave him a hug.

"Happy birthday, Pierre," I said.

"Drink … eat … dance," Pierre said, lifting his own glass. "We will be here all night."

A gorgeous young woman came up beside him and they walked off together.

"This is amazing," Claudia said, gazing at the people silhouetted in the light of the fires, the colorful lights overhead, and the tables of food and drinks. "I feel like we've been transported back to the seventeenth century."

"I feel like we're back in Africa," I said, gazing up at the full moon.

"Let's see what kind of food they have," she said and took my hand.

"You can't possibly be hungry?" I asked.

"Not a bit," she said. "But we can look."

A variety of cheeses, olives, pates, salads, caviar, breads, and French pastries, covered the tables

"If you want some meat," a man told me. "Take your plate over to the fire. They will give you some."

"*Merci*," I said, but couldn't think about eating.

Around us were platters of delicious foods, but my mouth was essentially taped shut. Nothing else was going down there this evening.

"Let's find Marius," Claudia suggested.

We set off across the lawn in search of the third birthday boy.

After giving our birthday wishes to all three young men, we were free to wander around the lawn, drinking, eating, dancing, and talking to new acquaintances. The problem was that nearly everyone else seemed to know each other. Claudia and I didn't know anyone other than Ruben, Pierre, and Marius. We strolled around for a while, drank champagne, and slowly wandered over to the spit with the roast pig.

You want some?" asked a man turning the spit.

Claudia looked at me and gritted her teeth.

"We should at least try it," I said. "How often do we get to eat roast pig at a party in a French chateau?"

"Never," she replied.

The man gave us each a small slice. When I popped it into my mouth, it was the most succulent pork I'd ever tasted.

"Oh my gosh," Claudia exclaimed, holding her fingers up to her lips. "Can you believe it?"

"No." I laughed. "And I'm too full to eat any more."

"Me too," she said. "And I'm tired. Can we go now? We still have to walk back to the RER and it's almost midnight."

So ended our weekend of the three best dinners we'd experienced during our time in France. They involved interesting people and conversations, cultural customs, ways of paying respect, and a lavish 17th century party.

"I can't believe we live in Paris," Claudia said as we walked up the narrow road to Versailles.

We laughed and then held our stomachs as we walked beneath the darkened trees.

Above our heads was the full moon; always an old friend and a promise of things to come.

Chapter 13
Café La Palette

Once you've lived in Paris for a while, you begin the search for your own café. It is more than a place to buy a coffee or a croissant. Your café is a refugee, a sanctuary, a convenient place to meet friends, or to sit in quiet introspection. It is an extension of your life; especially when you live in a small apartment where it is difficult to hold social gatherings.

We visited many cafes in our quarter and around the Place de la Republique, the Marais, and the Latin Quarter. But we hadn't yet found one that suited us. We weren't interested in the famous cafes on the boulevards, but preferred smaller, less known places. I had found one–the Café Au Grande Turenne on the Boulevard du Temple. It was a cheerful café with a pleasant terrace and only a few minutes from our apartment. I often went there to write letters or to read a book while Claudia was teaching. However, it was out of the way for our friends. We needed a place that was central to our life, and that meant a café somewhere near the Place de l'Odeon. I say *near* the Place de l'Odeon, because the square itself was far too busy with traffic and pedestrians to offer a comfortable, quiet café.

Still, we were always on the look-out.

By this time, we had met another couple who were to become our closest friends in Paris. Glen was an American lawyer who worked at La Defense. His girlfriend, Catherine, was from the Loire Valley. He was thin and energetic with a shock of dark curly hair–possibly from his Irish heritage. Catherine was small and reminded me of the French actress Juliette Binoche. A mutual friend introduced us at a party. Though it took us some time to get together, once we did, the four of us hit it off tremendously. Our first meeting was at the Number 10 bar on the rue de l'Odeon. It was a convenient location because Glen and Catherine lived in the 16th Arrondissement and we, of course, lived near the Place de la Republique. I often wondered as I walked up the street to the bar how many times Hemingway had strolled up this same sidewalk on his way to Shakespeare & Company.

One evening after dining out with Glen and Catherine, the four of us strolled along the Boulevard St.-Germaine. We had shared an excellent meal of hot scallop salad, lobster in spinach and mushroom sauce, fresh bread dipped in olive oil and pepper, and red wine. Afterwards, we all needed a walk and to take in the fresh air.

There were many street performers along the boulevard that evening, including a man who wore a Scottish beret and had a monkey on his arm, a blonde girl singing Edith Piaf songs, and a man giving hand-puppet shows.

Turning onto the rue de l'Ancienne Comédie, we passed Le Procope, the famously historic and now touristic restaurant that dated back to 1686. A round sign by the door stated that Napoleon Bonaparte and Benjamin Franklin had eaten there. As we strolled on, several humorous questions came to mind. Where had they gone to the bathroom while dining out in those days? If I stepped inside Le Procope now, would I find the same waiters, or perhaps the same napkins? Would I be able to tell the waiter, "Just give me what Ben Franklin had?" or should I be more culturally sensitive and say, "I'll have the Napoleon luncheon special?"

Down the street was a corner pub with tables set out on the sidewalk. A crowd of robust and heavily intoxicated young men–possibly an athletic team-stood outside. They were shouting and waving beer bottles in the air and we paused for a moment to watch. At the same time, a young man and woman stepped off the curb and walked toward the pub. The girl was slender with long, honey-blonde hair and the man had his arm around her. They looked to be in their early twenties; perhaps university students.

As they passed the pub, oblivious to the rowdy actions of the sidewalk crowd, a green beer bottle sailed out of the air and struck the girl in the forehead. The bottle broke on impact and cut her badly above her left eye. Her legs gave out and she crumpled to the pavement as if stuck with a hammer.

The young man charged back to the crowd.

"Who did this?" he shouted furiously. "Who? WHO DID THIS?"

He swung around as if to strike someone, but what could he do? No one confessed to having thrown the bottle. The group gazed back at him with drunken indifference.

"To hell with you!" he shouted. "To hell with all of you!"

Claudia raced over to the girl, who had revived and was holding her bloody head and crying.

It was impossible to know who had thrown the empty bottle, or even from which direction it had come. I imagined one of the drunks had tossed it thoughtlessly. Who would want to injure this innocent young woman?

A waiter from the pub rushed out with a handful of napkins and Claudia pressed them against the young woman's gashed forehead.

"*Merci*," the young man kept saying. "*Merci Madame.*"

He glared hatefully at the crowd, who seemed to have forgotten him and the girl and were once again shouting.

"Not so nice, eh?" Glen said to me.

"No," I replied. "Did you see who threw it?"

He shook his head.

Claudia stood up and wiped her hands on a napkin.

"I could use a drink now myself," she said.

"Oh, not here," Catherine protested.

"No, no," we all agreed.

We walked down the street until we reached the rue Jacques-Callot. On the far corner was the Café La Palette. It was dimly lit with outside tables beneath a white and green awning and looked quaint.

"Looks like a nice place," Glen said.

We agreed. The evening air was turning cool, so we stepped inside.

The café was warm and comfortable. Directly ahead was a long wooden bar and a narrow front room with tables. A passage on the right led to a back room lined with old paintings. I felt like we had stepped into a café from the 1920s or even earlier. Later, I learned that Paul Cezanne, Pablo Picasso, and George Braque had frequented this café.

The four of us sat at a table in the back.

"This is my kind of café," I said, gazing around.

"You've found a home," Claudia said and laughed.

A middle-aged waiter with dark curly hair came over to us. He wore a starched white shirt, black vest, black slacks, and a white apron.

"*Oui?*" he asked.

"What kind of dark beer do you have?" I asked.

"Grimbergen brune," he said. "From Belgium. *Tres bien.*"

"*J'en aurai un,*" I said, ordering one.

"*Moi aussi,*" Glen said.

Claudia and Catherine ordered Kir Royales-a French cocktail consisting of crème de cassis topped with champagne and served in a flute glass.

The waiter did not write any of this down, but nodded and hurried off.

We were talking about the young woman's injury from the beer bottle when the waiter returned. Without a word, he set the two frothy pints of Grimbergen in front of the girls and gave Glen and me the Kir Royales. I glanced up at him, ready to complain, when I saw a twinkle in his eye.

"I make the joke," he said and smiled.

We laughed and he hustled away. Throughout the evening, I watched as he darted from table to table, taking orders and serving drinks. To my surprise, he never wrote anything down. This waiter had a remarkable memory.

The following Friday evening the four of us visited La Palette again. This time the night air was warmer and the cobble-stone terrace was lit with a string of white lights. Two accordion players stood at the curb playing old French tunes. We seated ourselves at one of the outside tables. A few minutes later, the same waiter came over to us.

"Two Grimbergens and two Kir Royales?" he asked.

"Yes," we all said, amazed.

"*Bien*," he said and hustled off.

A bus girl was cleaning a nearby table.

"What is that waiter's name?" I asked.

"François," she replied.

"He has a fantastic memory."

"Oh," she said and shrugged. "He has been here forever."

From that evening on, we visited La Palette at least once a week, and especially on Friday evenings after Glen and I played squash. We would meet the girls and celebrate another victory for me on the squash court; at least, until Glen began to take lessons from a pro. Then I had no chance. We also held a surprise birthday party for Catherine in the back room amid the paintings.

François was always there and he always remembered our orders, no matter how crowded the café. The girls did not always have Kir Royales, although I always ordered a draft of the Grimbergen brune, as it was the best beer I'd ever tasted.

I hoped the young woman struck with the beer bottle had recovered quickly. It was an unfortunate ending to what I imagined had been a romantic evening for the couple. In the long run, however, it had led us to our café because Claudia had needed a drink after tending to the girl's wound. Without the flying beer bottle, we would probably have continued to the Place St.-Michel.

One evening I asked François how he remembered all those orders.

"Ah," he said and lifted his dark eyebrows. "I regard the face and recall the drink."

"It's a wonderful gift," Claudia said.

"It's a wonderful café," I said.

"*Bien sûr,*" François said. "*C'est La Palette.*"

Chapter 14
Kalyna's Solo

As the autumn passed, my wife picked up one part-time teaching job after another until she was working at the English Language School, the International Refugee Council, and at *L'ecole primaire* in Montmorency-a northern suburb of Paris. She found the differences in these teaching positions exciting, and would often come home with stories about incidents that had touched her or made her laugh. The quality of the student lunches at *L'ecole primaire* amazed her. Unlike so many stateside schools where students gobbled fish-sticks or a slice of pizza, students in Montmorency sat down to a delicious multi-course dinner with chicken, beef, or fish, vegetables, potatoes, and some type of pastry for dessert.

"They care about what the children eat," she said. "Wish I'd gone there when I was young."

"You'd never have fit in," I offered. "You're too much of a non-conformist."

"I would've tried," she replied thoughtfully. "For those lunches."

Although I still taught a full schedule at the English Language School, I applied for an evening class at the refugee school to supplement our income. I didn't realize the effect the new position would have on me. Working with refugees who had escaped political repression to find a better life in the West proved considerably more rewarding than working with bored French office workers.

Mr. Hagerty, the International School Director, was an Irishman with neatly trimmed white hair, soft blue eyes, and a gentle smile. I thought of him as a kind of saint. During our first conversation, he gave me a warning.

"Don't let the refugees get to you," he said. "They have such sad stories. It's bloody difficult to live under Communist rule. They'll break your heart and then you won't be able to teach. I've seen it happen a dozen times."

"I'll keep my distance," I said.

"But not too far," Elsie Wallace, Mr. Hagerty's assistant, urged. "Alec tells his teachers not to get involved, but these poor souls need someone who cares."

"So, you see the dilemma," Mr. Hagerty said. "Be nice and get close to your refugee students, but not too close. It's a fine line."

"And of course, they always *want* you to get close," Elsie said. "Imagine if you'd left your country and were living alone in a foreign city. Wouldn't you crave friendship?"

"I guess so," I said.

The refugees in my evening class were mainly from Eastern bloc countries, although we had a few from Vietnam. Some worked as maids or maintenance workers for wealthy clients in the 16th Arrondissement during the day, so they enrolled in the evening classes. We got along well and I enjoyed the work. They were eager to please, but didn't put much effort into studying. After all, they told me, Paris was just a stop before they reached their true destination – the United States. It would be easy to learn English there.

"Perhaps," I said. "But the more language you learn now, the less you'll have to learn later ... and the better you'll be able to get along."

Three weeks into the term, a new student appeared in class. She was a dark blonde with pale skin and brown eyes. The contrast between her naturally blonde hair and her dark eyes and eyebrows was striking.

She came up to the desk and handed me her entrance slip.

I read the form. She was nineteen years old.

"Kalyna?" I asked.

"Yes," she replied. "This my first class."

"Welcome," I said. "Where are you from?"

She glanced around the room and then leaned forward and whispered, "Kiev."

She had the sensual, aloof quality of young European women, and yet there was an underlying seriousness about her-the way her gaze flitted nervously around the classroom, the way she held her mouth–as if she wanted to say more but was afraid, and the way her slender fingers moved nervously over the edge of her notebook.

"Kiev," I repeated, trying to remember my one word of Ukrainian. "*Nasdorov'ya.*"

This was a drinking toast that meant *to your health.* Perhaps inappropriate in this setting, but I was grasping for anything that might make her feel more comfortable.

"*Nasdorov'ya,*" she said, correcting my pronunciation and looking at me curiously.

I motioned for her to take a seat and we began the class.

Two evenings later, Kalyna stayed behind when the other students left the classroom.

"You are American?" she asked shyly.

"Yes," I said.

She glanced around the empty room. "We can talk?"

"I'm heading to a café to meet my wife and get something to eat," I said. "Would you like to join us?"

She nodded.

Pedestrians dotted the Boulevard Haussmann. Claudia was already at the café and seated at an outside table. The evening air was getting cooler, but not so cool as to sit inside. I introduced Kalyna. A waiter came over and we ordered drinks. I also ordered a sandwich.

"You are from San Francisco?" she asked my wife, her tone hopeful.

"No." Claudia laughed. "It's a beautiful place, but expensive."

Kalyna gazed at a passing bus. An advertisement on the side of the bus announced a concert of Beethoven's music.

"I wish to go there," she said.

"San Francisco?" Claudia asked.

Kalyna nodded.

"Do you have friends there?" I asked.

She shook her lank blonde hair. "I wish to play in the symphony."

"The Symphony?" I asked. "What instrument do you play?"

She smiled shyly. "The flute. In Kiev I was soloist for the Youth Symphony Orchestra of Ukraine."

She explained this was not the same as the Kiev Symphony Orchestra, which was a professional organization. The Youth Symphony Orchestra was for young musicians who had not yet auditioned for the Kiev Symphony.

"We'd love to hear you play," Claudia said. "Maybe you could bring your flute to class some evening."

"If I am still here," Kalyna replied. "I wait for someone from Kiev. He can maybe arrive next week."

"Who are you waiting for?" I asked.

She drew back and glanced at her watch. If I had pulled out a Russian KGB badge, I don't think she would have reacted any differently.

"I must go now," she said abruptly. "Thank you for coffee."

"You're welcome," I said. "See you on Thursday."

She gazed up the boulevard and then hurried back the way she had come. We watched until she rounded the corner.

"She's cute," Claudia said.

"Guess I asked too many questions."

If Kalyna was waiting for someone from Kiev, then whoever it was had not yet left–or escaped–from the Ukraine. It reminded me of Peter and Tanya's story. I assumed there were Ukrainian informers in Paris, so why should this young refugee trust me? She had only met me a few times in English class.

It was still early evening and the sky was clear, so we walked down to the Quai des Tuileries and watched the *bateau mouche* floating tranquilly up the river. I loved watching the boats with their soft lights reflecting off the dark water. When we reached the Boulevard St.-Germain, I heard someone call my name. It was Mark Paley, another teacher.

"Finish your evening class?" he asked.

"Always a challenge," I said.

"How about joining us? We're going to a new café."

Every Tuesday evening Claudia and I went to a café with the other teachers. They were a fun group, always gossiping about other Americans who lived in Paris, having lengthy discussions on politics, and even more important–discovering cheap places to eat. If a teacher mentioned a restaurant and we asked about it, they would inevitably respond, "Oh, it has perfectly good food."

This meant the restaurant had medium quality food and was inexpensive, the much-sought-after type of eatery for our limited budgets.

"Who's *us*?" Claudia asked.

"Brigitte and Meg," Mark replied. "I'm supposed to meet them at nine."

Brigitte was Mark's French girlfriend. Meg was American and funny.

"Good," I said. "I could use a laugh."

"Something wrong?" he asked.

I shrugged. "I asked one of my refugee students too many questions and put them off. I feel bad about it."

"Oh, that happens all the time," Mark said. "They don't trust anybody. You have to get used to it."

The boulevard pulsated with heavy evening traffic.

"Where's the café?" Claudia asked.

"Two more blocks," Mark replied.

As we strolled along, I thought about Kalyna. I imagined it was too late in the evening for anyone to practice a flute, but she might be studying her music, gazing out her window and dreaming about San Francisco, or she might be at the Gare de l'Est, waiting patiently for a mysterious passenger to step off the train from Kiev.

"Here we are," Mark announced as we approached the Café La Palette.

"We come here all the time," I said.

He looked disappointed. "No, you don't."

"Every Friday," Claudia stressed.

"So, it's okay this time," I said, grinning. "But you have to promise you won't come back." (I was paraphrasing Hemingway here.)

"Gees," Mark huffed.

François the waiter came over to our table.

"Grimbergan?" he asked me.

"*Oui*," I replied.

"And a Kier for Madame?"

Claudia nodded and grinned at Mark.

"I've lived here two years," he scoffed. "How could you possibly have found this café ahead of me?"

"We get around," she said and laughed.

In addition to keeping a fine line between myself and the refugee students, I also learned not to make assumptions about them. The *He* Kalyna had referred to was not a boyfriend as I had imagined, but her Uncle Maxim who was escorting her two younger sisters to France. It was this trio of refugees who were supposed to arrive-someday-at the train station.

I discovered this a few weeks later when Kalyna arrived in class accompanied by two young women and a stout man with thinning brown hair and a dark moustache. The young women resembled Kalyna with their blonde hair and dark eyes and eyebrows.

"This my Uncle Maxim and my sisters Olena and Nina," she explained.

"From the train station?" I asked, afraid once again of overstepping my position.

Kalyna smiled, showing a dimple in her left cheek I hadn't noticed before. "Please forgive me to not answer. I was ..."

"It's okay," I said. "I understand. You must be careful."

Olena was sixteen and not as attractive as the other two girls. She regarded me sourly. Nina was thirteen and still childlike, with an adorable grin. I loved her immediately.

"Maybe you teach them English?" Kalyna asked.

"We'll get them signed up tomorrow," I said.

Uncle Maxim removed a cigarette from the corner of his mouth and shook my hand.

"*Dyakuyu*," he said.

I looked at Kalyna.

"He is saying thank you," she explained.

With her two sisters and uncle now in Paris, Kalyna was like a changed person, alight with a charming smile and a new sparkle in her eyes.

It was an interesting study to work with three sisters. Kalyna was intelligent and learned English with a little study. Being only thirteen, Nina picked it up quickly. Olena, in contrast, struggled with the language and was resentful of her sisters' accomplishments. I wondered if she regretted leaving Kiev.

The girls attended class until the new year. After the vacation, they did not return and although it surprised me, I was happy for them. I hoped they had made it to the United States. I could picture Kalyna seated in the San Francisco Symphony with flute to her lips, her blonde hair combed stylishly on either side of her face, and her striking eyes focused on the sheet music. In the audience, her sisters and her uncle would listen intently to melodies that sounded so much better when filtered through the soft air of freedom.

"Remember," Elsie had said. "Keep your distance, but not too far. These poor souls need someone who cares."

I think I handled the line appropriately. Especially with Uncle Maxim, who accompanied the girls to class each evening and managed to bum a few coins off me for cigarettes.

Chapter 15
La Comédie-Française

I was seated in a laundromat on the rue St.-Sebastien when an English couple entered. Claudia and I took turns doing the laundry and today was my turn. I didn't mind sitting in the warm silence, listening to the steady hum of the machines, and reading a book while the clothes rumbled in the washer and then the dryer. It was pleasant and reminded me of my college days.

This morning, I was writing an article for the Paris Free Voice on a new production of *A Midsummers Night Dream* that was scheduled to open in six weeks. I had interviewed the producer and director and attended a few rehearsals. I found the experience interesting–and not simply because the actresses who played Helena and Hermia were so talented. I enjoyed seeing how they blocked a play and rehearsed. Now I was scrambling to get the feature done because Rob had moved up the deadline to tomorrow morning.

The laundromat door gave a jangle and a couple entered. The man was thin and pale with shaggy brown hair. His wife had short-clipped dark hair and wore too much makeup. A filter-tipped cigarette jutted from between her polished red fingernails. Her costume looked far more expensive than the worn clothes of her husband, who might have been a professor of history or something. I could imagine how their relationship worked. She had probably helped his career socially and never let him forget it. He was an amiable but unpublished professor who liked to take a sip now and then to relieve the pressure of his home life. Why this unlikely duo was entering a laundromat in our quarter, I couldn't imagine. The 11th arrondissement was a working-man's borough. Perhaps they were staying at a hotel on the Place de la Republique and had gotten lost.

Then I saw a plastic bag dangling from the man's hand. It was crammed full of dirty clothes. They were customers.

Walking over to a washing machine as if it might be dangerous, they studied it carefully.

"The damned instructions are all written in French," the man said, exasperated. He had an English accent.

"Certainly, they take pounds," the woman said. Her accent was also English. "This is Paris, after all … an international city."

"Perhaps we should ask someone," the man said.

As I was the only other customer in the laundromat, they both swiveled toward me. I could feel their eyes scanning me from my scuffed leather shoes, blue jeans, navy-blue sweater, to the scarf tied around my neck. I could see them thinking, trying to determine if I was someone who could help, someone they could trust.

I smiled weakly, not wanting to get involved. I needed to finish my article. Fortunately, the woman dismissed me with a shrug and turned back to the machines.

I gave a sigh of relief. I wasn't important.

At that moment, the Portuguese laundromat manager came from the back of the shop. She was pushing a cart stacked with packets of detergent. I had seen her interact with customers before and knew she could be irritable. I set down my pen and watched, expecting fireworks.

"Pardon me," the man said. "Might we use pounds in these machines?"

The manager released her cart and it rolled a few feet on the scuffed linoleum tile. She looked at the man and then at the woman.

"No smoking," she grunted.

The English woman held up her cigarette. "I've nearly finished," she said. "Be patient."

"No smoking," the manager said again.

The English woman rolled her eyes. "God help me. Must we go through this, Donald? Let's just chuck the clothes and buy new ones."

"You know French clothes don't fit me, Sylvie," Donald grumbled. "I'm far too large."

I couldn't think what standard he used to determine that he was *far too large*. He was a thin, unhealthy-looking man; probably a smoker, from the gray pallor of his skin. But he was right about the French sizes. I could sometimes find a hat or jacket that fit me, but I didn't have a chance with shirts or trousers. They were simply too small.

Being larger than the average Frenchman had its rewards. When crammed into the Métro during rush-hour, I could usually see over the other passengers' heads. Since I was claustrophobic, this gave me a psychological advantage; a small area of breathable air-though it smelled like body odor and exhaust fumes.

"No smoking!" the manager said for the third time.

The English woman made a face. "Oh, bugger off," she snapped.

"Eh?" the manager asked.

Rising to her full height of five-foot-two inches, she glared at the English woman. Then, with jaw set firmly, she turned and stomped back toward the laundromat office. Stomping was hard to do because she was wearing a pair of those gray felt shoes all the cleaning women wore.

"No sense in reprimanding her darling," Donald said.

"You sod-off too," Sylvie replied. "This isn't the Hilton. We're in a bloody laundromat."

A moment later the manager's husband came out of the office. His face was flushed. The English couple was already off to a terrible start with him.

"What you say?" he asked in a huff. He was a short man with dark hair and a ragged growth of beard on his chin. I got the impression he only shaved once a week, probably on Saturday evenings before he took the missus out for dinner.

"Listen," Donald said. "We would like to use the washing machine. Do you take pounds?"

He pronounced these words carefully, as if the Portuguese husband spoke English quite well, but was a bit slow.

"Go!" the Portuguese man shouted.

From my experience, I didn't think the manager's husband spoke French very well. Now he was trying to speak English, and this was probably one of the few words he knew.

For the English couple, however, it was electric.

"Oh, for heaven's sake," Sylvie snapped. "Can we use the bloody machines or not?"

"Go!" the Portuguese man shouted again, and gave Donald a shove.

"Don't push him!" Sylvie yelled, whacking the man on the shoulder.

The manager's husband wheeled on her, his cheeks trembling with rage. He might have done her some harm, except at that moment the manager's bull terrier charged out of the office and bit Donald on the ankle.

"Ah!" Donald exclaimed. "The damned dog just bit me!"

He shook his leg, but the dog held on. It was a thick dog with small eyes and its white teeth sank into Donald's trouser leg as he scrambled to get away. The little mutt meant business.

My dryer had stopped. Normally I folded our clothes at the laundromat. There were several long tables in the back for this work, and it was always best to fold them while they were still warm. But I was in a hurry to get home and finish my article, so I scooped the clothes from the dryer, dumped them into the laundry basket, and headed toward the door.

As I stepped outside, the English couple, the manager's husband, and the bull terrier were still battling it out in a comic tussle between the machines. The manager had rushed out to support her husband and was smacking Donald across the back with a towel.

You couldn't make this kind of thing up. No one would ever believe it had happened. I shook my head and suppressed a chuckle until I got outside. Then I burst into laughter and raced home to tell Claudia.

Of course, I'd had my own conflicts with shop owners. In any large city you eventually run into clerks, servers, or administrative people who aren't friendly. Some are downright rude. But generally, we found the French to be extremely hospitable. They were so used to brash Americans who expected them to speak English that if you tried to speak French, they would do anything to help you.

Well, almost always.

One Sunday evening in early February, Glen and Catherine invited us to dinner at their apartment. When we arrived, Catherine was making spaghetti.

"We only have a little beer," she called from the kitchen, pronouncing 'little' as *leetle*. "If you want more, you must buy some."

"You want beer?" Glen asked.

I nodded. "I can get it."

"I'll go with you," he said.

The weather had turned cold and rainy. I pulled up my jacket collar as we walked down the street.

"There's a place around the corner," Glen said.

We stepped inside and shook the water from our jackets. A girl behind the counter had been arranging a box of cigarette lighters. When she saw us, she froze in mid-arrangement and fixed us with her dark eyes. Never had a shop clerk gazed at me with such hostility. Had she mistaken me for someone else? Was the store closed?

I glanced at my watch. It was half past seven. A sign on the door said the shop was open until eight o'clock on Sundays. We still had thirty minutes.

"I'll get some Kronenbourg," Glen said. "What beer do you like?"

"Pelforth," I replied.

We found the beer aisle. The six-packs were in bottles. I preferred bottles, but Glen liked his beer in cans; possibly a throwback to his St. Louis days.

"This beer is very expensive," he said to the girl in French. His tone was not critical, but surprised. He had lived in Paris for several years.

The girl's shoulder slumped, her head cocked, and she gazed at us with total contempt.

"Do you want it or not?" she asked.

An older woman stepped from behind the curtain. She resembled the girl right down to the same disdainful attitude. This had to be her mother.

"Do you have cans?" Glen asked.

"No," the girl muttered.

This was obviously not true. I could see a shelf of canned beer directly behind her.

The mother leaned forward aggressively on the counter.

"Make up your mind," she barked. "We're closing."

Glen glanced at me and raised his eyebrows. I looked at my watch again. According to the sign, we still had twenty minutes. How long did it take to buy beer?

"What time do you close?" Glen asked.

"Soon!" the woman snapped. "It's Sunday!"

Glen was a lawyer and it showed now.

"If you don't like to work on Sundays," he said. "Why are you open?"

I was grinning.

"What?" the woman cried. "What?"

She darted behind the curtain and shouted, "Pierre! Pierre!"

A man burst out from behind the curtain. I wondered how many people were back there. Perhaps a grandpa would leap out next, or perhaps a Doberman.

"They are being rude to me!" the woman shouted, nearly in tears.

Pierre was broad-shouldered, though paunchy. I tensed in case he took a swing at us.

"And they are foreigners!" the girl shouted. "FOREIGNERS!"

We were all frozen in silence for a moment: the three of them glaring at us with undisguised hostility, and us feeling completely innocent.

Then Glen said calmly, "We'll buy our beer someplace else."

We stepped outside. It was still raining.

"Can you believe it?" he asked.

"You *are* the typical rude foreigner," I said.

"What about you?"

"I try to fit in. I'm sensitive to all cultures."

"Bullshit," he said and laughed as we walked up the street.

When The Paris Free Voice published my *A Midsummers Night Dream* article, I read through it and remembered the English couple battling with the Portuguese manager, her husband, and the bull terrier, plus the obnoxious shop owners shouting that Glen and I were foreigners! It all fit together somehow.

Then I remembered what Puck had said in the play.

"Lord, what fools these mortals be!"

Chapter 16
Madame Remy's Pigeons

Yellow leaves lay scattered like dashes of captured sunlight on the Boulevard Voltaire as I gazed out my apartment window. A woman was feeding pigeons on the small square across from the Métro Oberkampf. When a German Shepherd raced up, the pigeons winged into the air with a swish of gray and white feathers, only to settle again after the dog had passed. A man in a colorful African *boubou* walked leisurely along the boulevard, hands clasped behind his back and an amused smile on his face as he chatted with a companion. In front of the *boulangerie* a woman was talking to a white poodle. The dog sat on the damp pavement and gazed up at her. I could imagine the woman saying, "Not now Fifi. You've already had enough pastries for today."

On the rue Crussol, a girl with braided hair, brown leather boots, black jeans, and a bulky sweater, was carrying an art drawing board. Her breath came out in timid, misty puffs as she passed through the chilling shade on the far side of the street. The golden afternoon light settled on the windows, balconies, and shutters of the apartment buildings on our corner of the rue de Malte.

"It's time," I muttered and glanced at my watch.

An old man came shuffling down the sidewalk. He wore a weathered snap-brim cap and clutched a burlap bag in one hand and a cigarette (perhaps a *Gauloises*) in the other. When he reached the corner, he glanced both ways and then crossed to the area near the kiosk where the woman had been feeding the pigeons. Had she known why he was there, she might have refrained. Because each afternoon he scattered seed around the corner and then stood back as pigeons fluttered down from the surrounding rooftops.

For a long time, I didn't know the identity of the man, but I appreciated this act of kindness and looked forward to seeing the pigeons flutter down each afternoon, their slate gray heads bobbing around the small chestnut tree near the kiosk.

Eventually, I learned he was the *portier* who handled minor repair jobs and some custodial duties in our building. I never heard his last name, but his first name was Gustave. He was hired by Madame Remy-who lived on the third floor-to throw out seed so she could watch the pigeons from her apartment window. She lived alone, one of the thousands of elderly citizens of Paris, tucked away in the ancient, cramped quarters of a city where so much of life was geared toward those with energy and hope.

My wife was returning from the *boulangerie* one morning when she saw Madame Remy struggling with the front door of our apartment building. The heavy wooden door was hard to open for someone clutching a grocery bag in one hand.

Claudia held the door as Madame Remy entered and then escorted her up the steps to her apartment. From that time on, they became friends and got together occasionally for tea, as our apartment was across the landing.

"Do you know she smokes cigars?" Claudia mentioned one day after a visit.

This struck me as comical. I could not picture the frail French woman sitting in her chair by the window and puffing away on a fat stogie.

"Not big ones," Claudia said. "They're small, almost like cigarettes."

I had to laugh.

Another time:

"Madame Remy knew Picasso! He stayed at her farm once. She has a ceramic figure he made and signed for her."

"I'd like to see that," I said.

"I'm sure she would show it to you."

And still later:

"Madame Remy's husband and son were shot by the Germans in World War II."

"She told you this?" I asked.

"Yes," Claudia replied. "Can you imagine?"

We learned that when the war broke out, Madame Remy was living on a farm in the Loire Valley with her husband and teenage son. Henri and Daniel were working in the fields one day when a convoy of Germans passed. Without warning or provocation, a truck stopped and several soldiers jumped out. The father and son remained beside their plow, wondering what the soldiers were doing. Possibly the convoy needed to ask for directions. But as Henri and Daniel walked toward the stone wall where the Germans waited, the soldiers opened fire. Madame Remy witnessed the killings from the kitchen window of her farmhouse.

"*Oh, non! Oh, Mon Dieu! Oh, non!*" she cried as she raced across the field, tripping as she ran over the uneven plowed ground. But there was nothing she could do. They were both dead.

Later in the war food became so scarce Madame Remy had to eat bread made from sawdust, and once even boiled up a broom handle.

Usually she spoke in the lilting Parisian French, which to my ear sounded like singing because of the rise and dip in pitch. From her lips the daily greeting of "*Bonjour, Monsieur,*" had the brightness and flow of a melody by Debussy. But if anyone brought up the Germans, her jaw would tighten and her gray eyes would flash.

"*Je deteste les Allemands!*" she would spit out. "I hate the Germans!"

"She's had such a sad life," Claudia said. "I wish there was something we could do for her."

"Like what?" I asked.

"I don't know ... something."

One evening as I was coming out of the Métro, I saw an ambulance parked in front of our apartment building. There is always a shock when you approach the place where you live and see an ambulance at the curb. My stomach tightened as I reached the door because something told me it was for Madame Remy. She had not been feeling well lately, and Claudia was concerned about her.

The front door was propped open and two attendants in white uniforms were hauling a stretcher inside. Claudia stood at the top of the stairs; her cheeks wet.

"It's Madame Remy," she informed me.

"I had a feeling," I said. "How is she?"

"She died."

The ambulance attendants wheeled the stretcher into Madame Remy's apartment. A few minutes later, they wheeled it out to the hallway and down the stairs. It hardly seemed possible that the slight form beneath the blanket was the kind old woman we had known. She had finally caught up with her husband and son, I thought with regret.

A few days after her death, I was surprised to see Gustave shuffling toward the kiosk with his burlap bag. The old man sprinkled the birdseed as usual and the pigeons fluttered down. I mentioned this to Claudia that night as we slipped into bed.

"Gustave was feeding the pigeons again this morning," I said. "I wonder who's paying for the birdseed?"

There was a pause and I watched pale streaks of moonlight come through the shutters and form lines on the bedroom wall. The lines reminded me of music, and music reminded me of Madame Remy's voice.

"I hope you don't mind," Claudia said at last. "I wanted to do something for her."

"You?"

"Yes."

I thought for a moment and felt her soft hair against the side of my face. It smelled of youth and dreams and tenderness.

"I'm glad you did," I said finally.
"So, you don't mind?"
"Not at all," I said.

Chapter 17
On the Quai de Valmy

The weather in Paris changed one weekend from brisk clear autumn to wet chilly winter, penetrating our clothes and causing us to tremble. People tramped along the sidewalks beneath dark umbrellas, jumped onto buses, or darted down the Métro's slick wet steps. The colorful café umbrellas in the Place St.-Michel were taken down and the awnings supplemented with plastic-sheeting walls and heaters. The cold weather and rain drove everyone inside, so that the cafes were crowded and some of the jazz clubs were so smoky you couldn't see the musicians performing. Now when you entered a café and didn't properly close the plastic covering so that the cold damp wind entered, customers at other tables would grimace and say, *"Mais non!"* or *"Pas encore!"*

I became adept at sprinting from the Métro Oberkampf to the awning of a kiosk, then to the overhang of a corner café and so on, darting here and there as I worked my way along the street to our apartment building in the rain. It wasn't the cold so much as the dampness that got to you. The constant in and out of the Métro left you feeling cold and then hot, and then cold again. You learned how to dress in layers–taking off jackets and sweaters or scarves as needed. Because once you caught a cold in Paris, it lingered for weeks.

Having moved to Paris from Africa, Claudia and I needed cold weather accessories like hats and gloves. We found these at the Galeries Lafayette, and afterwards stopped at an open-air food market. As we walked among the stalls, we filled our sacks with vegetables, eggs, dates, cheese, apples, a chicken, sausage, olives, and everything else we could find and afford that looked appetizing.

Beyond one stall a *clochard* (or street person) sat on the curb with a piece of cardboard beneath him. He held up a sign asking for food money. He was incredibly dirty and his long greasy hair hung down in his face. The two jackets and sweater he wore were in tatters and smudged with grease and filth. He wore old shoes and blue jeans stiff with grime.

His sign read: *J'ai faim. L'argent pour la nourriture s'il vous plaît.* (I'm hungry. Money for food please.)

We felt sorry for him because he looked so miserable sitting there in the rain. There were so many *clochards* in Paris. You often saw them on the rue de Rivoli, hunched over the heating vents in the sidewalks.

On the corner was a sandwich stand.

"I'll get him something," Claudia said.

She bought a turkey, lettuce, and tomato sandwich on a fresh Kaiser roll and took it to the man. When she offered it to him, he pushed her hand away.

"He doesn't want it," she said, amazed.

This confused me at first, and then a realization came to me. "Maybe he gets the food he needs from people who leave portions of their sandwiches or dinners here in the market."

"But he says he's hungry," she said.

"Yeah," I said. "But maybe not for food."

"You mean what he really wants is to buy wine or liquor ... or whatever?"

"Would you give him money if his sign said he wanted to get drunk?" I asked.

"So sad," she said.

When we got back to our apartment, Peter and Tanya were waiting on the curb. They were toting guitar cases.

"We play something for you," Peter said in his halting English.

"Come up," we said.

We had spent a lot of time talking with them about bluegrass music and how much they enjoyed it, but we had never heard them play. Now, after a moment of tuning up, Peter placed his guitar across his right knee, glanced at Tanya to see if she was ready, and launched into a bluegrass tune called *Hornpipe.*

I was astounded. They were fantastic.

Their fingers moved in nimble unison up and down the frets and the music they produced seemed so authentic and so amazingly wonderful, it was difficult to believe they were from Prague and not the backwoods of Tennessee.

Claudia was grinning and clapping to the music. It was impossible not to be enthusiastic. Peter and Tanya played like professionals. They moved effortlessly from one tune to the next.

"Will you stay for dinner?" Claudia asked when they had finished.

They smiled delightedly.

"Very kind," Peter replied.

After dinner, Claudia made popcorn. She covered the bottom of a pot with oil and popcorn kernels and put on the lid. Then she set it over the flames of our gas stove to heat.

When the first kernel popped and struck the inside lid of the pan, Tanya leaped up from her chair.

"What?" she asked, frightened. "What is it?"

We laughed.

"Popcorn," I replied.

"What is popcorn?" Peter asked.

Now it was our turn to be shocked.

"You've never heard of popcorn?" Claudia asked.

They hadn't.

Tanya put her face close to the pan and listened to the popping, even opening the lid and allowing two kernels to eject onto the floor.

When the popping finished, Claudia dribbled on melted butter and sprinkled salt. She put it in a large bowl and gave it to them. Tanya's eyes lit up when she placed the popcorn into her mouth.

"Oh, my goodness," she said. "This is incredible!"

Peter's wide grin widened even more.

"Welcome to America," I said and we all laughed.

We bonded as friends that evening and saw each other frequently. I played the guitar too–although nowhere near their level–and Peter taught me how to pick a few songs. This eventually culminated in the two of us playing in the Métro.

I had often heard musicians performing in the Métro–especially around the larger stations. Normally, this consisted of a solo performer on a guitar or a saxophone. Once I heard a string ensemble playing Mozart's *Eine Kleine Nachtmusik*. The acoustics of the station made the music come vibrantly alive. Mozart would have loved it. But I hadn't thought much about the strategy of performing in the Métro until Peter suggested we try our hand.

"How bad could it be?" he asked. "No one knows us. If we are bad, we go home."

The truth of this brightened me considerably.

"Okay," I said. "I'll try."

We spent a long time discussing where we wanted to play. It had to be a location that wasn't too popular because we had only practiced together a few times. Also, it shouldn't be too small, because we hoped to make a few francs.

"You should play at the Métro Republique," Claudia suggested.

I looked at Peter.

He shrugged. "Fine with me."

The next Saturday morning, we found ourselves in a tiled white corridor leading to the Châtelet platform. Slipping on our guitars, we played *Deep River Blues*. I was nervous at first. Then I realized the noise from the arriving and departing trains was so loud no one could hear us. It didn't matter how well or badly we played.

"Let's move," Peter suggested.

"Not yet," I said. "Let's get used to the acoustics."

He nodded and we practiced a few more songs.

Finally, we settled on an intersection where passengers were coming and going from two directions. There was more foot-traffic here and we could hear ourselves.

We played for nearly an hour. Many people smiled as they walked past, but no one dropped a coin into our open guitar case.

After *Blue Railroad Train*–one of my favorite Doc Watson songs, a teenage boy stepped up with a twenty-franc bill in his hand. I thought he was going to drop it into our open guitar case. Instead, he gazed at me imploringly.

"Pardon," he said, holding out the bill. "Have you change for the Métro?"

Half an hour later, a woman and a little girl stopped to listen. The girl tapped her foot and bobbed her head to the music. We had an audience! Our playing became more enthusiastic.

After a rollicking version of *Tennessee Stud*–me playing rhythm and Peter doing the picking and singing the English lyrics in his thick Czech accent, the woman came toward us. Smiling, she reached into her pocket.

Here it comes, I thought, grinning–our first donation.

When her hand came out, however, she was holding a Métro map.

"Excuse me," she said. "Can you help me with directions to Bellville?"

So ended our career as Métro musicians.

The chilly rain had settled in one evening when Tanya appeared at our door. Hanging her raincoat on a hook in our entry, she paced across the living room. From the look of concern in her eyes, I wondered if something had happened to Peter. I'd seen her happy, contemplative, even angry, but never like this.

"What's wrong?" I asked.

"I received a note," she said. "From a friend of my father."

"That's good," Claudia said.

"Perhaps," Tanya said. "Perhaps not. It could be a trap."

"What do you mean?" I asked.

She explained that the man wanted to meet her at an apartment building the next afternoon. He had something to give her from her family.

"It could be the Czech secret police," Tanya said. "It's been done before. You go to the apartment and they grab you."

"So don't go," I suggested.

She paced to the wall where three French posters we'd purchased at a stall by Notre Dame hung, and turned back again.

"I don't know what to do," she said, biting her thumbnail. "Perhaps he really is a friend of my father."

I didn't know what to tell her. This was way out of my experience. "So ..."

"Will you go with me?" she asked.

"Me?"

"Yes."

I lifted my eyebrows and glanced at Claudia. She shrugged. This was cloak and dagger stuff. It seemed surrealistic.

"What about Peter?" I asked.

Tanya pushed the damp hair back from her face. "We can't risk both of us going."

"Right," I said.

"You don't have to go into the apartment," she offered. "You can wait on the street. If I disappear, I want someone to know what happened."

"Of course," I said.

She breathed out slowly. "We'll see."

We met the next afternoon in front of an apartment building on the Quai de Valmy. It had stopped raining, but the wind was damp.

146

The canal was behind us. I looked to see if any boats were docked in the water near the building; especially ones with a covering. Since my job was to assume the worst, I was trying to imagine how they would get her out of Paris. Probably they would drug her and take her out in the trunk of a car.

The canal was clear. No boats.

Tanya lingered on the sidewalk and gazed up at the third-floor window. She bit the inside of her lip and paced back and forth in her knee-length boots. Finally, she shook her head.

"I can't do it," she said. "It doesn't feel right. Let's go."

Without another word, we hurried down the street. We didn't stop until we were six blocks away, and then we darted into the Métro Jacques Bonsergent and boarded the first train.

I had always taken Peter and Tanya's escape from Prague seriously, but standing outside the apartment building on the Quai de Valmy gave me a better understanding of the fear they had experienced crossing the Czech border, and the real danger through which they had passed. Tanya didn't mention her appointment with the man in the apartment building again, so I'll never know if he really was a friend of her father or if it was a trap. But I do know one thing—the danger felt real.

Chapter 18
Riding the Métro

Parisians have an expression for their daily working life: "*Métro, Boulot, Dodo.*" This is *Argot Français* for the daily repetition of taking the Métro, working, and sleeping.

I thought of these words as I took the Métro to school each morning, finding myself packed into a coach with dozens of other riders, everyone standing because there wasn't room to sit—and if there was, you didn't take the seat because then you would be too far from the door when you reached your stop. Trying to push through a packed coach of swaying bodies before the doors closed again could be a challenge.

Usually, I enjoyed the Métro because it was direct and, in a city where it rained so often, pleasant to tramp down the steps and into the dry comfort of the station. Also, the Métro was a wonderful place to people watch. As we sped along the darkened tracks, I liked to determine the passengers' nationalities, get a sense of who they were by their age, how they dressed, what they carried, or their expressions. Many passengers affected a blank expression—no life in the eyes, nothing to give them away or attract attention. Their body was seated across from you, but their thoughts were somewhere else – far away from this dull mode of transportation.

At least, that's what they wanted you to think. In reality, the passengers often glanced at each other from the corners of their eyes, determining if the person seated across from them was safe. If not, they would casually change seats or get off at the next stop and change cars.

This happened to me. Just as the coach doors were closing one day, a man jumped aboard. He looked wild–with unkempt, tangled hair, a shirt that was unbuttoned and loose, and a crazed look in his eyes. There was no doubt this guy was trouble.

149

He stood inside the door for a moment and then walked up and down the aisle, yelling about something in an incoherent language. As he yelled, his actions became increasingly violent. This wasn't going to end well, I thought, and watched as passengers at his end of the coach slowly moved away.

I wondered what people would do if he attacked someone, which seemed very plausible. He was swinging his arms as if punching invisible enemies and shouting, with spittle flying from his lips. When we reached the next station, many of the passengers in my coach got off and scrambled into an adjacent car. I wasn't far behind. I had things to do and wasn't in the mood to hassle with a lunatic.

Beggars were also frequent in the Métro. You often saw Middle Eastern women dressed in robes, carrying sleeping (possibly drugged) babies, and asking for money. The uniformity of their hand-written signs made me wonder if someone else organized and controlled them; and the coins they earned weren't simply going for food money.

One evening Claudia and I went to a movie on the Avenue des Champs Elysees with Hailey Barrow. We arrived early and were first in line at the ticket window. The wait was only fifteen minutes, but by the time the young woman behind the glass was prepared to sell tickets, we were about ten people back. The French are not as ruthless at this as the Sicilians, who will literally push you out of the way–especially when food is concerned; but first one and then another person squeezed between us until we were far back from our original position at the window.

After the film, we had a drink at a café and walked to the Métro George V. From there, we caught a train to the Hôtel de Ville and changed to the Mairie des Lilas line. As we traveled farther away from the Avenue des Champs Elysees, the passengers in the coach changed in appearance and economic status.

I sat across from Claudia and Hailey and couldn't see what was happening behind me. Apparently, a young woman with spikey orange hair had entered our coach at the Rambuteau stop. She was dressed in black leather with lots of silver zippers.

Claudia smiled at her and this infuriated the girl. Gazing fiercely at my wife, she took out a little penknife, opened the blade, and strapped it up and down the back of the seat behind me. This gesture was apparently supposed to intimidate Claudia. Instead, Claudia laughed and nudged Hailey. Now orange-head jabbed at the air with her little knife, all the while making sneering expressions of hatred.

"Oh, c'mon," I heard Claudia say, but didn't know what she was talking about, unaware of the drama playing out behind my back.

At the next stop the girl got off, sticking out her pierced tongue as she stepped onto the platform.

The doors closed and Claudia burst into laughter.

"Did you see her?" she asked me.

"Who?" I asked.

"The girl with the orange hair."

"No."

Claudia held her sides, laughing. "When she got out that little knife …"

"I'm thinking of having my hair done that way," Hailey said, and grinned.

Claudia didn't care how anyone wore their hair. Her intentions were friendly when she smiled at the girl; but the young woman didn't take it that way–or possibly thought we looked too bourgeoisie. Anyway, it was the threatening penknife that Claudia found amusing.

We reached our stop and the doors opened. As I was stepping off the coach, I felt a tug on my back pocket. I knew instantly what was happening.

Only a few weeks earlier, I'd been given a leather wallet. It was nicely crafted, but large. When I slipped it into my back pocket, it stuck up about an inch. I knew better. The Métro lines, tourist areas, and the Latin Quarter were crawling with pickpockets. Groups of gypsy children would surround a person and pick them clean, even as the victim tried to swat them away. There were also plenty of individual thieves, and now one had his hand in the back pocket of my jeans.

Fortunately, his timing was off.

Whipping around, I grabbed his wrist. He dropped the wallet and jumped back. I snatched it up and shouted, "VOLEUR!" as the alarm buzzer sounded and the coach doors closed. The train pulled away and I could see passengers in the coach staring at him.

As soon as I got home, I changed wallets and from then on carried a smaller wallet in my front pocket. But other friends found themselves targets. The worst was a friend who had her money and passport stolen while praying in Notre Dame Cathedral.

Chapter 19
That Cold Mountain Air

Snowflakes floated outside our chalet window in Montriond, a ski resort in the Auvergne-Rhône-Alpes region of France.

"Who's next?" Francois asked.

"Claudia," Nicole whispered.

"Bring her in."

We all suppressed chuckles as Monique led my wife blindfolded into the dining room.

The chalet where we were staying was nestled into a small valley with a steep rock cliff on one side and a slope of Swiss stone pines on the other. It had ten bedrooms on the upper floor and a large kitchen and dining area on the ground floor.

That morning we had skied along a scenic trail to *Lac de Montriond* and then up to an old inn and restaurant. A heavy white mist hung over the frozen expanse.

On the far side of the ridge was a shanty at the top of a long fast drop to the lake. Claudia took the slope first. She was an experienced skier and handled the downhill plunge smoothly, only slowing when she got to the tree line. I, on the other hand, was a novice and hoped I could make it on pure effort, or stupidity, or perhaps luck. I pushed off.

When the slope became too fast, I tried to do a half-snowplow with my left ski. The ski caught on a chunk of ice and I spun, falling onto my back, and sliding headfirst down the slope.

Claudia laughed as I brushed snow from my face and jacket.

"Don't put so much pressure on the ski," she said.

"Give me till Wednesday," I replied. "I'll make it then without spilling."

"It's a bet," she said.

We were sharing the chateau with four French couples from Normandy. After skiing, we ate a hearty dinner of roast chicken, mashed potatoes, salad, bread, and cheese. We accompanied this with wine, and shots of bourbon to warm us.

We were all in fine spirits now, so the evening games had started.

As Monique led Claudia into the dining room, Gerard pulled off his shirt and leaned forward over the table. I took Claudia's right hand and folded her fingers so that only her index finger pointed out. Then I ran it slowly down Gerard's bare back. As her fingertip touched his backbone, she flinched.

"Oh, gees!" she gasped.

Her fingertip moved across his skin. She was nearly down to his waist now.

"What're we doing?" she asked.

I didn't reply, but kept moving her hand until she reached Gerard's lower back. Monique was waiting with the half orange. Nicole had carved a hole in the center of it.

Just before Claudia reached Gerard's jeans, I lifted her finger and plunged it into the orange.

"AHHH!" she shouted, jumping away and pulling off her blindfold.

We exploded into laughter.

"That is *so* gross!" she cried.

Monique had tears on her cheeks from laughing so hard.

Claudia gazed at her.

"You're as *dégueulasse* as Nicole!" she yelled.

Nicole had a crude sense of humor and adored disgusting jokes.

"Do you think so?" Monique asked.

"Yes!" Claudia snapped.

A delighted grin spread across Monique's face.

"Oh, thank you," she said.

When it was Colette's turn, she chased Gerard around the dining room, trying to wipe her finger on his cheek.

We laughed until we cried.

In the morning the northern peak outside our window was yellow with cold early light. Claudia wanted to go alpine skiing with some of the group, so I walked her to the lift. Then Gerard and I took a hard-packed cross-country trail that led for five kilometers into the mountains. It became warmer as we climbed and I removed first my ski jacket and then my sweater until eventually I was skiing in my tee shirt.

We passed a group of old barns known as the *Mine D'or*. The barns smelled sweet and warm inside. There was so much snow on the roofs you could ski over them. From this vantage point we could see for miles. It was a wonderful feeling to be up so high. The sky was blue and the sun glittered off the snow.

On the return we made the steep, slick, winding five-kilometer descent. At the bottom my ankles ached, but I felt good and exhilarated that I hadn't fallen. In fact, I felt better than I had in months: healthy, rested, sound, and mentally clear.

Later in the day as the sky grew dim and a gray mist settled on the mountain peaks and pine trees, Claudia and I went out for another run. There was no one else on the slopes and a heavy silence only deep snow can create filled the woods.

"I wanna try it again," I said.

"The shanty run?" she asked.

"Yes."

"It's getting dark," she said. "Be careful."

We skied up through the woods to the ridge. As I stood poised at the top, I couldn't decide if the slope looked easier or more difficult in the gray mist.

"See you at the bottom," Claudia said and pushed off.

I watched her pink and blue ski jacket rush down the slope and disappear into the mist.

Okay, I thought. Now was the time. She would be down to the lake trail by now.

Crouching, I pushed off.

It was a rush to be flying down a hill in the half light. It reminded me of a time in Africa when I'd ridden a motorbike after too many beers. The motorbike seemed to disappear beneath me, and I felt as if I was flying as you do in dreams. It was a pleasant feeling. Now I was floating down a winter slope in Morzine.

As I picked up speed, I saw the gray stone wall and bridge on my left. Here the trail dropped steeply and I couldn't hold it. The skis when out from under me, and I fell hard on my right side. My right ski caught in the snow and I felt a sharp pain in my ankle. I spun to a halt on my back and lay gazing up at the flakes coming down through the pines.

"Are you okay?" Claudia asked.

"My ankle hurts," I replied.

"Do you think it's broken?"

I felt down within myself.

"No ... maybe sprained."

This was conjecture on my part. I'd never broken a bone and I wondered about this, because my father had been a reckless youth with an older brother who had often gotten him into trouble, including being hit by a car and diving off a roof. My father used to say that (thanks to my Uncle Bud) he'd broken nearly every bone in his body at least once. I knew this was an exaggeration, but some of it was true. You only had to look at the bump where he'd broken his nose. That was the time Uncle Bud had raced down a hill with my father on his handlebars.

"How could I have known a truck was coming?" he had asked.

To avoid the truck, Uncle Bud had turned his bicycle hard to the right, running into the curb and sending my father flying head-first into a wooden fence. He may have broken his left arm too that time, but I get it mixed up with the time the car hit him. In that second incident, my father was also perched on Uncle Bud's handlebars. He always believed it when Uncle Bud said everything was going to be okay and that they would have fun. Uncle Bud was his older brother and my father not only trusted him, but looked up to and admired him. In fact, he always believed right up to the minute the doctor put the cast on.

Fortunately, we were on the lake trail now and the path through the woods to the chalet was flat. I tried not to put pressure on my ankle as we skied.

When we reached the chalet, I pulled off my ski boot and socks. The ankle wasn't swollen, but ached, so I kept off it for the rest of the evening.

At least until after dinner.

"*Bon,*" Colette said, holding up a length of cord.

The ten of us had eaten a dinner of roast beef and green beans, and were still seated around the dining table.

"When the end of the cord arrives to you, you must put it through a piece of your clothing. *D'accord?*"

We all nodded.

The cord made its slow journey around the table, passing up sleeves, through sweaters, under jackets, and various pieces of clothing. When it reached me, I ran it through a belt loop on my jeans and passed it to Nicole, who slipped it through one arm of her sweater and then passed it to François. When the cord had at last gone the full circle of the table–ten people in all–Colette tied the two ends together in a tight knot.

"Now," she said, grinning. "To get up from the table, you must remove the piece of clothing attached to the cord."

"What?" we gasped.

Gerard knew the game and had passed the cord through his wrist-watch band.

"Haha," he said, laughing as he pulled off his watch.

Monique had not been so prudent and had to remove her blouse.

We went around the table in this way, some people embarrassed and others delighted by the removal of their clothing. Claudia had passed the cord through the arm of her sweater, but she was wearing a thin turtleneck top underneath.

Then it was my turn. I had passed the cord through one of the belt loops on my jeans.

This was going to get embarrassing.

As we crawled into bed that evening-the heavy covers feeling wonderful in the cold room-we heard a shriek from down the hall. Alarmed, I jumped up and dashed into the hallway. Colette was racing toward me, flailing at something with a broom.

"A mouse!" she cried.

A gray field mouse was scurrying over the wooden floor just ahead of her. It darted past my bare toes and down the stairs.

Colette ended her pursuit at the top of the stairs, gripping the broom with both hands and trying to catch her breath.

"A mouse," she gasped.

"You almost got him," I said.

She nodded. "Do you think he will stay downstairs?"

"I would," I said.

She giggled. "I don't like mice."

"Where's Lionel?"

I expected her husband to be with her.

"Snoring," she said and blushed. "It would take dynamite to wake him."

"Well," I said. "*Bonne nuit.*"

"*Bonne nuit,*" she said and padded back to her room in her wool socks.

I wondered where she had gotten the broom.

Claudia did not require dynamite to wake up. All that night she thought she heard mice under our bed. She imagined them scurrying and gnawing and squeaking. I didn't hear anything, and I was a light sleeper.

"It's okay," I said. "If there is a mouse, it won't hurt you."

"Do you hear it?" she asked.

"No."

We had spent a week in Africa sleeping in a rat-infested room and those large black rodents were nasty. A little field mouse trying to keep warm in an alpine chalet was no big deal.

"Listen," she whispered.

I lay there listening for a long time in the darkness–never hearing a mouse–and began to say something when I heard her breathing change to deep exhalations.

She was asleep.

On our last morning in Montriond, I peered out the window to see the pine trees and rooftops of the surrounding chalets deep in snow.

"Yes!" I exclaimed happily.

Grabbing our cross-country skis, we trekked up the mountain to a waterfall high above the town. Large ice blocks from an avalanche covered part of the trail. I was worried about Claudia as she made her way across, her skis on her shoulder. If she slipped, it was a long way down.

A narrow wooden footbridge spanned the waterfall. The snow on the bridge was higher than the railings. We each took our time, digging our boots into the snow with each step as we crossed and holding our skis for balance. Once across, we continued up the trail.

At the top were three barns and I stepped into one, imagining the cattle up there in the summer and the hollow sound of their cow bells as they grazed. The sky was blue and the snow was getting mushy. We skied through the pines and down the winding mountain trail. By the time we reached the shanty and the slope that had given me so much trouble on two previous runs – nearly spraining my ankle–it was dusk. This was the final descent. We would pack the car soon for the return trip to Paris.

Nicole and François took the slope.

Claudia stood beside me, tapping her ski poles anxiously into the snow.

"Forget the bet," she said.

I looked at her. "No way."

"How's your ankle?"

"Don't know," I replied. "I chopped it off yesterday."

"Okay, down-hill racer," she said, grinning. "I'll be watching."

She pushed off.

I was alone now and gazed at the lake below, the snow-dusted pine forests, the mountain peaks that seemed to blend with the gray sky, and the rooftops of Montriond. Taking in a deep breath of the pine-scented air, I let it out slowly.

Here I am, I told myself-skiing in France.

This was a promise I'd made myself on those sweltering lonely nights in Africa when we sat, surrounded by the oppressive isolation of the dry bush, and watched as insects flitted around our kerosene lantern.

Now I was here.

I didn't want to leave, but the others were waiting. Kicking my skis to knock off the snow, I crouched and pushed off. The first steep drop came up fast and then I was in the middle section near the stone wall and bridge. I held my balance and prepared for the second downhill grade that had wiped me out twice now.

Dammit, it isn't going to happen again, I told myself.

My right ski slipped a little but held and with a rush, I made it down the final stretch to the tree line.

Claudia clapped her gloved-hands excitedly.

"You made it!" she cried.

"Finally," I said.

"We must celebrate," François said, and pulled a flask from his ski jacket. Unscrewing the cap, he took a drink and handed it to me. The flask held peppermint schnapps.

"That reminds me of the dirtiest story," Nicole said with a grin.

"Oh, no," Claudia muttered.

We departed Montriond at nine o'clock that evening. As we left the Auvergne-Rhône-Alpes and headed northwest toward Paris, the snowfall outside the car window turned to rain.

Chapter 20
Richard Clayderman's Piano

We were driving through the Col de la Joux Verte pass from Morzine to the resort of Avoriaz when Gerard put on a tape of piano music. As the snow-covered chalets and white dusted pines of the French Alps rolled past my window, the piano's lilting sounds enchanted me. The music fit perfectly with the slopes of the Portes du Soleil ski area.

"Who is this?" I asked.

"Richard Clayderman," Gerard replied.

"He's good."

"Yes," Gerard said. "Very popular in France."

As I was to learn, Clayderman was a French pianist who played sophisticated arrangements of original and popular music. The album now playing was *Lettre à ma Mère*.

I had contradictory feelings about French music. For me, the true music of France was Edith Piaf singing *Je Ne Regrette Rien* or *La Vie En Rose*. But it was also the cool Paris blues of the 1950s. In contrast was the embarrassing attempt of Johnny Hallyday to present himself as the French Elvis.

Now here was Richard Clayderman performing entertaining, intelligent music that seemed to fit the time. Along with the incredibly beautiful music of Michel Legrand, it was the beginning of a new musical trend in France.

Shortly after our return to Paris from Morzine, I got word that my friend Patrick was in town and trying to contact us. He was staying at the apartment of an American writer. I phoned and we made plans to meet the next evening.

When we arrived, the bar he had suggested was too crowded, so we walked around the corner to a larger cafe. Patrick told us he was traveling through Paris to the Himalayas, Nepal, Rangoon, and Thailand–a great far-east trek.

"Sounds exciting," I said.

He grinned. "I hope to write a book about it."

As we were sitting at the café–much to my astonishment–a Richard Clayderman song sounded from the speakers. A week ago, I'd never heard of this guy and now I was hearing his piano music everywhere.

"Isn't he from Paris?" Patrick asked.

"I think so," I replied.

Patrick grinned again. He had an easy-going, spiritual quality that reminded me of Somerset Maugham's main character Larry Darrell in *The Razor's Edge*. Like Darrell, Patrick was seeking more out of life that the shallow existence of wealth.

"I know where he records," Patrick said. "I have a friend who works there. Would you like to go?"

I nodded eagerly and bought the next round of drinks.

Delphine Studios was located on the rue Dr. Lancereaux near the Métro Miromesnil. I had never been in a recording studio before and was excited. Patrick introduced me to his friends Didier and Nicole, who worked as recording engineers. They showed me around. Pictures of Clayderman lined the walls.

"Let me give you some of his albums," Nicole said.

She gathered up a stack and handed them to me. I counted seven.

A beautiful grand piano sat in the studio.

"That's his piano," Didier said. "Would you like to play it?"

"Really?" I asked.

"Of course," he said.

I entered the studio, sat at the piano, and played several pieces I had composed myself. The keys had a firm touch. It was wonderful, and I played for about twenty minutes. When I looked up, Patrick, Didier, and Nicole were smiling.

"Did you see him?" Patrick asked when I returned to the sound booth.

"Who?" I asked.

"Clayderman. He was here ... watching you play. He just left."

"What?"

"You write your own music?" Didier asked.

"Well ... yes," I replied. "Though I'm more interested in lyrics. I always wanted to be the next Bernie Taupin."

Nicole laughed. "But of course."

A few nights later I got a call from Didier.

"A young French girl – Autumn White-is beginning her career," he said. "She has the potential for being a big star. Would you like to play some of your songs for her?"

Was he kidding?

"Of course," I said.

"*Bon,*" he said and gave me an address. "Be there at five o'clock tomorrow."

I didn't know what to expect when I arrived at Autumn White's apartment. When I tapped on her door, the experience was like the scene in *Notting Hill* when Hugh Grant visited Julia Roberts in the hotel. A young woman greeted me in French and escorted me to an inner room where I met Autumn's mother, Suzanne. People were rushing around everywhere. I couldn't imagine what they were all doing, but they seemed very busy and very determined.

Suzanne escorted me into another room and motioned for me to sit at a piano. This room was quiet and as I slipped onto the piano bench, I felt that I had reached the eye of the storm.

"Autumn will be here in a moment," Suzanne said and closed the door.

I tinkered with the keys for a few minutes until the door opened again and a teenaged girl entered. She was slender with soft brown hair and an impish grin. She also had a quality of being sexy and gritty. I imagined you had to be tough to make it in this business.

"*Bonjour*," she said. "You have the music?"

"Yes," I said, and handed her the charts.

I played three songs. Autumn liked one of them and sang along as I played. She had a wonderful voice.

Her mother stood off to one side and listened.

"Time for the photos," her mother said finally, glancing at her watch.

Autumn smiled and left the room.

"I like the last one," Suzanne said. "I will talk with Autumn and we'll get back to you. Okay?"

"Okay," I said.

Three days later I was told Autumn felt the songs were too old for her. I should have made the arrangements more in tune with her teenage style. Or I should have written a new song just for her. I had blown a golden opportunity.

She eventually came out with an album titled *Mais Si*. It was popular and I was happy for her.

That afternoon I rang Didier at Delphine Records and asked if I could come over and play Richard Clayderman's piano one last time.

"Yes, yes," he said. "No problem."

"Do you think he might be there?" I asked.

"Clayderman?" Didier replied. "No, he's on tour in Italy."

"Of course," I said.

Chapter 21
Teaching on the Edge

As I was crossing the Pont D'Arcole on my way to school, I noticed the air held a hint of warmth. It was after ten o'clock and the penetrating chill of the early morning had faded. The sun, glowing dimly through a thick cloud cover, was as bright as it was going to get. Pausing for a moment at the bridge railing, I gazed down at the Seine. The river was high and had flooded the bank roads on the levee. A cobble-stone walkway where only last week we had taken photos of the Île Saint-Louis was now under water. A line of colorful barges was docked farther upstream.

Gillian sat behind her desk in the school office.

"Feels like spring is coming," I said.

"That's what all novices to Paris say at this time of year," she replied. "Don't let it fool you. Winter isn't over yet."

"You're sure?" I asked with a smile.

"Quite," she replied.

In class one of my students had a nasty cut across her nose and a black eye.

"What happened to you?" I asked.

"I went skiing this weekend and fell face down," she said. "*Merde*, it hurt."

The gash across her nose might leave a small scar, but the Alpine sun had tanned her face and she looked healthy.

Another student told me she was studying English because she wanted to be a flight attendant.

"I imagine it will help you," I said.

"Oh yes," she said and transformed herself into an attendant now. "Good morning, ladies and gentlemen. Welcome to flight 407 to Tangiers."

She laughed joyfully and we all laughed with her.

There was a school staff meeting that evening. Jack Duffy's assistant ran these and they were usually a joke. I was fed up with schedule changes and the administration's lack of organization. When the meeting ended, I walked out without saying a word. I was crossing the inner courtyard when I heard Jack shout, "Goodbye!"

My cheeks flushed because, with all his faults, I liked Jack. He had always been fair to me. When I was having trouble with attendance in a class, he took me aside and explained the problem.

"The mistake you're making is letting your students know you *want* them to be in class," he explained. "The French take this as a form of weakness."

"Because I care?" I asked.

"Yes," he replied. "When they start playing games, tell them to kiss off and walk out. They'll respect you for it."

"Seriously?" I asked.

"Try it," he said. "You'll see."

When I got outside now, giving myself time to cool down, I phoned him.

"Let's have a drink," I suggested. "Thursday evening."

"What time?"

"Seven?"

Jack had a deep chuckle that sounded as if it was just waiting to escape.

"I feel like invitations are brought on by providence," he said. "I should always accept."

"Okay then," I said. "Café de l'Odéon?"

"See you there," he replied.

When I got home Claudia was already in bed. As I entered the room, she sat up and turned on her bedside light.

"I'm so glad you're here," she said.

She was trembling.

"What's the matter?" I asked.

"I had a rough time tonight with three refugees."

"What do you mean?"

After her class at the refugee school, Claudia occasionally went for drinks with some of her students. This is how she got to know Peter and Tanya.

While I was at the teacher meeting, she went to a café with her Romanian student Marius, his wife Alina, and their baby daughter. Claudia and Alina were chatting happily about babies, when three refugee students arrived, uninvited, and pulled up chairs. The young men had been drinking.

Claudia recognized two of them: Wiktor and Bartosz from Warsaw. She didn't know the third young man.

"So," Wiktor said, leaning across the table toward Claudia. "When are you going to let us into your precious United States?"

Claudia looked at him. She assumed he was making a joke, but he wasn't smiling.

"You know I don't have anything to do with that," she replied. "You have to apply at the embassy."

"I think maybe you do," Wiktor said. "I think maybe the embassy is asking for your recommendation."

Claudia gave a quick laugh. "They don't care what I think."

"And what *do* you think?" Wiktor demanded.

"Stop this," Marius said. "You're being rude. Claudia is a good teacher. She cares about us."

"Maybe you," Wiktor said, glancing at the baby. "So wholesome, so nice. But us …"

Claudia pushed back from the table. "I should be going."

Bartosz grabbed her wrist.

"You aren't going anywhere until you let us into your country."

Claudia pushed Bartosz's hand away.

"You want your passports stamped?" she snapped.

"Of course," he replied.

"Then leave me alone. One word from me to the embassy and you'll never get in. None of you!"

Marius and Alina nodded.

Bartosz released his grip.

"I thought so," Wiktor muttered.

Claudia left the café and hurried down the boulevard to the bus stop, listening for a rush of footsteps behind her, not knowing what she would do if they came. She didn't hear any. Apparently, her bluff had worked. Her legs felt wobbly. Sitting on a bench, she cried until the number 20 bus arrived and she hopped aboard.

I was furious with the Polish students and proud of Claudia for standing up to them.

"You have to tell Mr. Hagerty," I said. "Or I'll tell him for you."

"I'd rather discuss it with Elsie."

"Okay," I said. "But promise me you'll tell her. They need to know."

"Oh, I will," she said.

The next morning Claudia talked with the assistant school director about the incident. She never saw the three young men again.

After hearing her story, my petty complaints about schedule changes and lack of organization embarrassed me. They seemed egotistical and trite now compared to her experience. I decided that when I got together with Jack for a drink, I wouldn't mention school.

We met as planned at the Café de l'Odéon. The place was crowded, but we managed to wedge into an empty space near the stairs. We talked about writing and writers we admired. Jack believed you couldn't call yourself a writer unless you were on the best-seller list. He delivered a rowdy discourse on this subject while knocking back one scotch after another.

By midnight he was singing *You're the Top* by Cole Porter and jumping up and trying to smack a light bulb dangling from the ceiling.

When it was time to leave, he searched sloppily through his pockets and gazed at me with blurry eyes.

"I seem to have forgotten my money," he said, running his hands through his pockets again.

"That's okay," I said. "I got it."

On the street he rubbed his eyes with the palms of his hands and shook his head.

"My wife is going to be upset," he muttered.

"Why?" I assumed it was because of the drinking.

"We were going to a party this evening. I told her I wouldn't be long."

"Well, shit," I said.

Jack's wife was sweet and attractive, and I didn't want to be the cause of her disappointment. I should have suggested he go home sooner. I felt bad about this. But then again, he should have told me he and his wife had plans for the evening. Jack was like that. He was unorganized and irresponsible and easily distracted. For all that, however, you couldn't help but like him. He was a man of exuberant energy and spontaneity. Wonderful in a drinking companion; not so great in a boss. I could only shake my head as he walked up the street. I had offered to help him back to his apartment–he only lived a short distance away–but he thought it would be better if he returned alone.

When he was about halfway down the block, I thought I heard snatches of Cole Porter once again.

The next day was chilly with just a pale back-lighting of sun through the clouds. The hint of warmth in the air was gone.

"You were right," I said to Gillian when I arrived at school. "It's not spring yet."

"Not even close," she said. "The sun doesn't penetrate the clouds now until about half-past eight."

"I know," I said. "I didn't want to get out of bed this morning."

She smiled and gazed out the window.

"Me either," she said. "It's colder than a nun's fanny today."

Chapter 22
April Fish Day

In France, the first day of April is called April Fish Day. The derivation of this holiday is vague, but dates to 1564. As a gag, you're supposed to give someone a small gift – such as a chocolate fish, or to stick a paper fish on someone's back. If they don't notice, that's the joke.

I needed a gift for Claudia, so with an hour to spend before my first class, I walked over to the Place de l'Opera. The sidewalks were crowded. On the granite steps of the Opera building, people were sunning themselves. I continued to the Place Vendome and the Ritz Hotel. For being famous, the place was bleak and lacked charm, so I headed back up the boulevard.

I perused shop window after shop window but could not find a fish. So, in desperation, I entered a flower shop and bought my wife a potted plant. I felt ridiculous walking up the street carrying the large pot, and even more so when I entered my classroom and set it carefully on the desk.

"You like plants?" one of my Bulgarian students asked.

"It's for April Fish Day," I explained.

"It's a fish plant?" another student asked.

I laughed. "No, it's just a plant. I wanted to buy a chocolate fish for my wife, but couldn't find one."

"So, you got her a plant?" a young Polish woman asked with concern.

"Not a good idea?" I asked.

She shook her head.

"What kind is it?" asked another.

I moved the plant to the center of the desk.

"It's called a Peace Lily."

The lady at the shop had said it was easy to grow and tolerated low or medium light, which was what we usually got in Paris. I liked its glossy foliage and white flowers.

"Don't you think the flowers look a bit like fish?" I asked the young woman.

She shook her head again and gazed at me with pity.

When I got home at lunchtime, I was surprised to find two familiar faces in our apartment. Laura and Joe had just arrived from Brittany.

Claudia greeted me at the door.

"Look who just turned up," she said with forced joviality.

I handed her the Peace Lily.

"Happy Fish Day," I said and gave her a kiss.

"What's that?" Joe asked.

I explained the tradition.

"And you're giving her a plant?" Laura asked.

Claudia went into the kitchen and returned with something behind her back.

"Happy Fish Day," she said and handed me a chocolate fish."

"That's more like it," Laura said, laughing.

I was tired of them already and it hadn't been ten minutes.

"They're staying until Thursday," Claudia explained, gazing at me with her lips tight.

"Five days, huh ... wonderful," I replied.

Joe slapped his hands together. "What do you want to do?"

"We could walk around the Latin Quarter," Laura suggested. "Maybe get lunch at one of the local bistros."

We had known her for years; first in the states and then in Africa. We had only met Joe a few times since their marriage. My first impression of him wasn't favorable. On their last visit, he hadn't told us he was a vegetarian until we were seated at a popular seafood restaurant. He also struck me as being inflexible. I found inflexible people difficult to be around.

Joe sprang up from the couch.

"I know," he said, ignoring Laura's suggestion. "Let's go to the horse races at Auteuil."

I knew the horses were running that afternoon. I turned to Claudia. "Is that something you'd like to do?"

She smiled. "No, but that's okay. You boys go. I'll bake chocolate chip cookies."

"Mmm," Joe murmured.

"What about me?" Laura asked.

Joe looked at her. "Stay with Claudia."

Laura folded her arms and gazed at him with her jaw clenched. She was doing everything but tapping her foot.

Uh oh, I thought.

"We could all go," I suggested.

"Yes," Claudia said, taking in the situation. "I'll bake the cookies later."

Joe looked disappointed. "I thought it was just going to be us guys."

"This will be more fun," I said.

While the others got ready, I ran down to the kiosk and bought a racing paper. On the Métro to the Porte d'Auteuil, I studied the paper and circled my choices. By the time we reached the track, the sky was partially cloudy and the wind had picked up, though it was still a pleasant day.

I started out by hitting three winners in a row. They were favorites and didn't pay much, but it was fun to cheer them on. Joe wasn't winning anything because he liked to go for long shots.

"You get more money that way if you win," he explained.

"But you're losing," Laura said.

We both lost on the next two races and then I won again on the sixth. I wasn't getting rich, but I was winning enough to buy us dinner and was having fun.

Joe, on the other hand ...

Laura was in tears.

"Why are you doing this?" she asked. "You're not only wasting your money, you're blowing mine."

"Maybe we should go," Claudia suggested. "I can make the cookies and ..."

Joe spoke up. "I'm not leaving until I win a race!"

"You'll never win!" Laura snapped. "You're not a winner!"

"Says who?" he shouted.

I took him aside.

"Listen," I said. "Everybody has bad days. Save your money and we'll come back."

Joe looked at me. "What she said wasn't cool."

"She's upset," I offered.

We left the track and endured the long cold ride home in the Métro. When I say cold, I'm not talking about the ventilation system of the underground. I'm talking about the wall of ice between Laura and Joe.

When we reached the apartment, a note from Hailey was tacked to our door. She and a group of our friends had gone to dinner at the Hippopotamus Bar on the Boulevard Beaumarchais. They invited us to join them.

I glanced at my watch. It had only been twenty minutes since Hailey had left the note. We could catch them if we hurried, and I very much wanted to go. I needed a break from our guests.

So did Claudia.

"We'll catch a taxi," she said.

Rushing out to the Boulevard Voltaire, we flagged down a cab.

"The Hippopotamus Bar," Claudia said to the driver as we all piled into the car.

"*Oui Madame,*" he said.

Spinning the taxi around, he headed up the boulevard toward the Place de la Republique.

"We're going in the wrong direction!" I shouted. "Beaumarchais is back there!"

Claudia patted my knee. "He knows where he's going."

"But there's more than one Hippo Bar," I said. "The one we want is near the Bastille."

"Maybe there's a traffic jam," she replied.

I settled back into the seat, put a hand to my chin, and gazed at the passing scenery.

Ten minutes later, the taxi pulled up to the Hippopotamus Bar on the Boulevard des Capucines. The driver turned and gazed at us, a grin on his face.

"I thought you said it was on the Boulevard Beaumarchais," Joe said.

"It is," I replied.

"So, this isn't it?" Laura asked.

"No."

"He made a mistake," Claudia said.

"Evidently," I said.

We explained to the driver that we wanted the Hippopotamus Bar on the Boulevard Beaumarchais. His smile faded and he gave us a disgusted look.

"*D'accord,*" he muttered and wheeled the taxi around again.

It was raining by the time we reached the restaurant, which seemed appropriate for the mood of the evening. I paid the driver and we hurried inside. Our friends were gathered at a corner table and were happy to see us. We were pleased to see them. Claudia made the introductions and we sat down.

After a few minutes a waiter came over and took our orders. Laura said she wanted the steak burger with grilled bacon, onions, tomato, lettuce, and cheddar cheese on a brioché bun.

Joe put down his menu and gazed at her.

"They have veggie burgers," he said.

Laura glanced at him but didn't speak.

"It's better for you and ..."

Now she was staring at him. "What?"

"It won't make you fatter."

"You bastard," she said.

The table went silent.

"I'm only saying," Joe continued.

Laura dropped her menu on the table, closed her eyes, and let out a long sigh.

"Okay," she said finally. "Give me whatever he's having."

"*Deux Salade Paysanne,*" the waiter said.

When it was served, I had to admit the salad looked appetizing with grilled bacon, sliced hard-boiled eggs, and chunks of baby red potatoes over mixed salad in a vinaigrette balsamic dressing.

But it wasn't what Laura had wanted.

Joe and Laura stayed with us for five more days. It was a long visit and during that time, I frequently checked to see if I had a paper fish stuck to my back.

Chapter 23
Light from the Eiffel Tower

As I stood on the Place de la Concorde, waiting for Claudia to arrive, I glanced across the river to the Eiffel Tower rising above the trees. The morning had begun overcast and cold, but now the day was crisp and sunny. In fact, the sun was arced so precisely in the sky that it seemed to shine from the top of the tower. It was a wonderful image and I smiled. It reminded me of the scene in *Indiana Jones and the Lost Ark* where the sun hit the medallion Jones held on a stick and showed the precise location of the ark. Only now the precise location was the Place de la Concorde and there was no hidden ark, but only the beauty and clear brilliance of Paris.

"Are you ready?" asked a voice.

Claudia was standing beside me, grinning in her delighted way. Hailey Barrow was with her.

The girls had asked me to meet them outside the Hôtel de Crillon. Hailey had a friend who lived nearby, and they had spent the afternoon visiting her. Now the idea was to buy me a leather jacket as a brace against the sharp Paris chill–not that we could afford to purchase anything in this quarter.

Apparently, it was going to be a team effort.

For weeks I'd been trying to find a jacket in the various department stores, but to no avail. Either I didn't like the style or none of the jackets fit. Hailey suggested we try the Leather Marche near the rue de Temple.

It took us two bus rides to reach the market from the Place de la Concorde. Sometimes – especially when the weather was clear–we couldn't bear to slog down into the smelly, white-tiled Métro. On those days, we preferred to take a bus, and reveled in the passing streets, shops, and pedestrians we couldn't see from underground.

179

The Leather Marche was a large warehouse filled with row after row of tables piled high with leather goods. It resembled the leather markets in Florence, Italy. I was certain I would find a jacket here. As the three of us entered, we were immediately accosted by vendors trying to attract our attention.

No one ever mistook me for a Frenchman. I was taller than the average Parisian, plus I had reddish brown hair and blue eyes. Usually, they assumed I was Dutch or Belgian. The rare clerk thought I was Canadian. As a result, the vendors approached me with a variety of languages. However, as soon as I replied in French, they relaxed and the discussion of prices began.

"Two thousand francs," a vendor said, holding up a jacket.

We had learned to bargain in Africa and knew that when it came to local markets, it was best not to show any interest and to never be in a hurry. This second lesson had proved especially important in Istanbul when we shopped for rugs at the Grand Bazaar. The Turkish vendors invited you to sit, have a cup of tea, possibly introduced you to their family members, and then discussed the rugs. The same was true of the French vendors—only on a smaller scale; no tea offered here, but time was not pressing.

We moved on to several other tables.

Hailey grew impatient.

"I didn't realize this was going to take all afternoon," she huffed. "I'm going to find a pastry and some coffee."

She worked her way through the tables to a bistro on the far side of the market.

Claudia laughed. "She isn't used to shopping in Abidjan."

"We're pros," I said.

Claudia held a jacket up to my back for size.

"Try this one," she suggested.

I tried it on and it fit comfortably. The brown leather was soft and it had a brown cloth lining.

"I like it," I said.

Hailey returned with a croissant in her hand.

"Twelve hundred," the vendor said, skipping any small talk.

"Are you going to buy it?" she asked.

I took off the jacket and laid it on the table.

"Haven't decided," I muttered.

"Good leather," the man said, running his fingertips over the sleeve of the jacket.

"It looks good on you," Hailey offered.

"Thanks," I said and began to walk away.

"Okay, okay," the man said. "One thousand."

I picked up the jacket again and studied the zipper and the pockets. It was well made and exactly what I was looking for.

I put it down again.

"Oh, c'mon," Hailey moaned and took a bite of her croissant.

"Give him time," Claudia said.

"Six hundred," I offered.

The vendor looked startled.

"*Monsieur,*" he said, holding his palms up. "This is not possible."

"Let's go," I said to the girls.

We took a few steps up the aisle.

"Nine hundred," the vendor called.

"Seven hundred," I countered.

"Eight hundred francs," he said.

I turned and gazed at him.

"Eight hundred?"

"*Oui.*"

"Okay," I said.

He nodded enthusiastically as I counted out the money and placed it in his palm. Then he folded the jacket and handed it to me.

"*Merci,*" he said, tipping his snap-brim hat.

We moved off across the market. I was pleased with my new jacket and looked forward to wearing it in the cold Paris weather. I felt that I had made a good purchase, though I might have gotten a better price if I'd taken more time. In Istanbul, a good bargain is when you get the rug for a quarter of the original asking price. But I was content, and the vendor seemed pleased too.

Later, we ate dinner at a Chinese restaurant Hailey recommended. After a short walk, she led us down a flight of stairs and we entered through a fancy door into a large room. I would never have known a restaurant was on the block if Hailey hadn't shown us. The street was completely dark. Inside the restaurant, about a hundred people were seated at tables and eating dinner.

"This is amazing," Claudia said.

"Wait till you see how the food is served," Hailey said.

We found a table and a waiter took our drink orders.

"You see those little carts?" Hailey asked.

We nodded.

"When they come around, you see what looks good and make a choice. The waiter serves it to you."

"Great," I said. "I'm hungry."

Within a minute, a Chinese waiter rolled a cart over to our table. He lifted the bamboo lids off various dishes and explained their contents. His French was so heavily accented that I only understood about half of what he was saying. Nevertheless, we each selected an entrée and sat back while he served us.

"I'm not even sure what I ordered," I said.

"Twice cooked pork, I think," Hailey replied.

The drinks came and we relaxed. The food wasn't bad, whatever it was, and from the next cart I ordered a spicy beef dish with caraway seeds. Claudia ordered an asparagus dish in a brown sauce. We spent the evening sampling different Chinese delicacies and drinking Tsingtao beer.

Afterwards we were walking back to the Métro when I glanced into a passageway and stopped. Two baby elephants stood there, swinging their trunks, and eating straw. A trainer was with them. I couldn't believe it. This was the second time I'd seen elephants in Paris; both times unexpectedly.

"How many elephants are there in Paris?" I asked.

"I didn't know there were any," Claudia replied.

"I see them all the time," Hailey said, and laughed.

I thought about the afternoon beginning with the sun shining from the tip of the Eiffel Tower, the leather market, finding a jacket, eating mysterious and delicious Chinese food, making toasts with Tsingtao beer, and seeing elephants for the second time in Paris.

All in all, it was a nice birthday.

Chapter 24
Our Home and Native Land

"Can you help me with this tie?" Peter Bressler asked.

His fingers were trembling so that he was having trouble tightening the knot.

I might have laughed, except for the situation. He and Tanya were preparing for their interview at the U. S. Embassy. Peter had gotten his hair cut and looked sharp. The always beautiful Tanya wore a pink dress she had made herself. Neither of them had slept well the night before.

Their appointment was at two o'clock. It was now half past one.

"Maybe they will let us live in Tennessee or Kentucky," Peter said as he stood with chin up and let me adjust his collar. "We can play bluegrass there."

"I hope so," I said.

They had worked so hard and been so courageous to get here—risking everything to cross the border and reach freedom in the west.

"It was like escaping a prison camp," Tanya once said.

We were at a café only a few blocks from the U. S. Embassy.

"Ready?" I asked.

"Yes," they said excitedly.

Although Peter and Tanya were nearly shaking with anxiety as we headed toward the embassy, I was confident. Tanya had gone to a university in Prague and was a civil engineer. Peter hadn't been allowed to attend the university because of his father's defection, but he had become a trained mechanic in a hydro-electric-plant. They were young, intelligent, motivated, loved the United States, and had refugee status. I couldn't imagine why they wouldn't be accepted.

The embassy was on the Avenue Gabriel just off the Place de la Concorde. A gray military van was parked on the curb outside the gate. French soldiers in blue uniforms stood in clusters around the entrance. One soldier stood with the falling autumn leaves blowing around his black military boots. A carbine was slung over his shoulder and a walkie-talkie hung from his neck. He wore black leather gloves and looked cold in the crisp air.

I walked Peter and Tanya to the entrance and waited as they showed the guard their passports and signed in for the interview.

"I'll be here when you come out," I said. "We'll have some celebrating to do."

Tanya waved and they stepped through the gate and entered the embassy.

I was excited. This was going to be so much fun. I couldn't wait to see the joy on their faces when they returned.

The interview was expected to take about an hour, so I wandered around the corner to a café. Forty-five minutes later I was standing once again outside the gate, waiting.

Promptly at three o'clock I could see them coming.

I pumped my fist into the air. This was the moment.

But something was wrong.

Tanya was sobbing uncontrollably. She rushed up and put her arms around me. I held her and felt her tears against my shirt.

"What happened?" I asked.

"We were rejected," Peter said.

"Why?"

He glanced back at the embassy guard. "I don't want to talk about it here."

"Let's go over to the Tuileries," I suggested.

We crossed the Place de la Concorde and entered the park. People were gathered in chairs around the fountain. Finding an empty bench, we sat down.

"His father has done it again," Tanya spluttered, wiping her nose. "The same old story."

When Marek had defected after the Prague Spring, leaving his family behind and settling in France, Peter was kicked out of school. Now the United States didn't think it was necessary for the young couple to leave France when Peter's father already lived here.

"Stay with your family," they were told.

"Peter wants a new life in America and he is held back again because of his father," Tanya said. "It isn't fair."

"There is always another way," I said.

"Like what?" Peter asked.

"I don't know," I said. "I'll have to think about it."

"Will you?" Tanya asked. "We can't stay here. This is not our country."

I gazed around the park with its gravel paths, fountain, and beautiful trees. Off to the right was the river and farther along the Eiffel Tower.

"Isn't Paris beautiful?" I asked.

"Yes," Peter replied. "But Prague is more beautiful."

"And we left Prague," Tanya pointed out.

"Okay," I said. "I'll try to think of something."

That evening Claudia and I went out to dinner.

"Why don't we write an appeal?" she suggested. "All our American friends can sign it. Maybe it will help."

"Great idea," I said.

Two nights later I came home to find her seated at our dining room table with Peter, Tanya, and Hailey.

"We've written the appeal," Claudia said. "Will you look it over?"

"We spent a long time discussing the language and attention to semantics," Hailey said. "It sounds very official."

Pouring myself a beer, I sat down and read the appeal. Hailey was correct. It did sound official. It asked the embassy to accept Peter and

Tanya's immigration status, and ended with an emotional statement about American justice.

"It's perfect," I said. "They can't turn this down."

But they did, and so quickly I couldn't believe anyone at the embassy had actually read the letter.

"Bastards," I muttered.

At the same time, a Polish refugee we knew applied for immigration status. Jozef was in his mid-twenties with long hair and a straggly beard.

"Do you think I will be able to get a job in the United States?" he asked me one day.

"What's your occupation?" I asked.

He grinned. "I was a rock drummer in Warsaw."

"No problem," I said. "The fast-food industry always needs people."

Unlike the Czechs, I didn't think Jozef had a chance of being accepted by the embassy.

I was wrong.

"I got in," he told me happily a few days later. "The quota for Polish refugees was not full, so I was accepted. Can you believe it?"

"No," I said, feeling sick.

My country had turned down two highly motivated, educated, wonderful young people and accepted an unemployed Polish rock drummer instead. I was embarrassed.

Then an idea occurred to me.

"What about Canada?" I asked.

I'd heard that Canada had a different immigration policy. Instead of simply filling quotas, they were looking for qualified immigrants who could help the country as experienced workers, rather than being a drain on the nation's benefits.

"Never thought about it," Peter mused.

"Once you're Canadians, you can travel to the states anytime you want," I said.

"Yes," Tanya said, and I could see her mind working behind the dark brown eyes. "Do you think it's possible?"

"Let's find out," I said.

The Canadian embassy was on the Rue Montaigne near the Champs-Élysées. It took two weeks to set up the appointment. I was supposed to meet them in front of the embassy at ten forty-five. At eleven o'clock, they still hadn't arrived. Then I saw them running up the street. When they reached me, they were both out of breath.

"Peter and that damned tie," Tanya huffed.

He had been trying all morning to tie his tie, but was too nervous for his fingers to work. Tanya's face was strained. After the big let-down of the U.S. Embassy interview, they really needed the acceptance of Canada.

"No pink dress?" I asked her.

"I'll never wear it again," she said, frowning. "Bad luck."

"My tie," Peter gasped.

"I'll fix it," I said.

Once they were presentable, I escorted them into the embassy. We waited in an outer room until they were called.

"You'll do great," I said.

Tanya smiled, but she looked nervous.

I waited in the outer room, getting up from time to time to pace across the hardwood floor and back again. The U.S. embassy denial had shaken my confidence.

Finally. the door opened and they came out. Both were grinning and Tanya had tears in her eyes—but they were tears of joy.

A gray-haired man with glasses escorted them. This was the Canadian administrator who had handled the interview.

"I see no problem with them immigrating," he said. "I'll personally help if I can."

"Oh, thank you," I said, shaking his hand. "This is fantastic."

"A remarkable young couple," he said.

We hurried from the embassy and met Claudia at the Gallery Lafayette. She had a delighted smile and her eyes sparkled.

"You look happy," I remarked.

"A French guy tried to pick me up while I was waiting for you," she said.

"This pleases you?" I asked.

"Of course. Every woman wants to be attractive."

She turned to the Czechs.

"Well?" she asked.

"They want us!" Tanya cried. "We leave for Winnipeg in three or four months!"

Claudia hugged them and when she pulled away, she had tears in her eyes.

I knew she would.

I wanted to ask her more about the French guy–what he looked like, what he said–but refrained. I was happy that she was happy. Things were working out for everyone. Peter and Tanya were going to Canada, and Claudia felt attractive.

Things were even working out for me.

She *had* told the guy *no*, after all.

Chapter 25
Poissons et Visiteurs

One thing that never changed during our time in Paris was visitors. During our first September on the rue de Malte, we had company every night except one. They came in ones and twos, were good friends, distant acquaintances, relatives of friends, relatives of distant acquaintances, and sometimes complete strangers. Sometimes they notified us in advance, and sometimes we had no idea they were coming until our buzzer sounded to let us know someone was downstairs on the sidewalk.

Once I went down to find an attractive blonde smiling at me as I opened the door.

"Hi," she said, holding out a hand. "I'm Karen's sister Megan."

She mentioned the name of a young woman we had known in Abidjan.

"I just got in from Amsterdam and wondered if you could possibly put me up for the night," she continued.

"Well ..." I said, hesitating. "I don't know what Claudia has planned for this evening. Why don't you come up?"

Megan grabbed her backpack and I held the door as she entered.

"Karen told me about your adventures in Africa," she said as we ascended the stairs. "It sounds so romantic."

I chuckled. "It was hot, dry, isolated, and occasionally dangerous. I never thought of it as romantic."

We entered the apartment. Claudia was studying a French grammar book at the dining room table. I made the introductions.

"Meagan wants to know if we can put her up for the night," I said.

Claudia folded her lower lip beneath her upper lip and nodded. I knew what that expression meant. She was going to say yes-even though it was the last thing she wanted. She and this girl's sister had been good friends; and in Africa, no visitor was ever turned away.

191

"Of course," she said, giving Megan a hug. "We'd be glad to put you up."

"Oh, thank you," Megan said. "I really appreciate it."

She gazed at us, her eyes moving from me to Claudia and then back again. "I hate to even ask," she said, grimacing. "But I have a friend with me. Could he stay too?"

We'd been hooked, and very professionally. I didn't respond.

"Okay," Claudia said wearily.

"Oh, thank you," Megan gushed, and hurried downstairs.

"He's here?" I asked.

"Yes," she called up. "He's waiting outside."

A moment later, a young man with stringy hair and a sprinkling of beard on his chin came up the stairs. He didn't look as though he bathed often, and I was reluctant to shake his hand.

"This is Dirk," Megan said. "He's from Rotterdam."

"*Hallo*," Dirk said, grinning.

"He's an artist," Megan persisted.

"What kind?" I asked.

"Drawings mostly," Dirk replied. "Perhaps I will sketch one for you."

We spent a pleasant evening sipping wine and reminiscing with Megan about our adventures with her sister. Dirk told us about growing up in Rotterdam. We mentioned that we had visited Corrie ten Boom's house in Haarlem. He had never heard of her, but he knew a lot about Rembrandt and Mondrian.

"You like Mondrian?" I asked.

"Naturally," Dirk replied. "He is an important Dutch artist. You don't appreciate his work?"

"I like his self-portrait from 1900," I said. "His other work ... not so much."

"Ah," Dirk mused. "That is because the self-portrait is impressionism. His later work is abstract art."

"You got me," I admitted. "I'm an impressionist at heart."

Our apartment only had one bedroom. Visitors slept on a couch in the living room that could double as a twin bed. If we had two guests–unless they wanted to share the twin bed–one of them had to sleep on the floor. We kept a pad for this rolled up in the hall closet.

We had to work in the morning, so we set out sheets and blankets and left Megan and Dirk to decide their sleeping arrangements.

When I tip-toed through the living room the next morning at half-past six, I found Megan in the bed and Dirk sprawled on the floor. He was sleeping on his stomach with his arms and legs flung out so that I had to step carefully over him as I headed to the kitchen. I made my breakfast as quietly as possible and then slipped out to the hallway, happy they would be gone when I returned that evening.

They weren't.

In fact, Dirk seemed to have settled in for the duration. His clothes lay scattered all over the dining area–on chairs, doorknobs, and even hanging from a window latch.

"So, they aren't leaving today?" I asked Claudia.

She shrugged. "Megan asked if they could stay one more night."

"Just one?"

She nodded.

But after the second night, it was obvious Dirk had no plans to leave. Drawings from his sketchbook covered the floor and he had stopped rolling up the sleeping pad when he woke in the morning. Now I had to watch my step anytime I walked through the living room. Both he and Megan were always present at dinner, but never offered to help clean up. And Dirk was beginning to smell especially ripe.

One evening when he had gone for a walk, Megan and I were talking.

"So … how long have you two been dating?" I asked.

She looked surprised. "We haven't. I met him on the train from Amsterdam. I hardly know him."

"What?" Claudia asked, coming into the room.

Megan shrugged. "I asked if he could stay here and you said yes."

I cursed under my breath.

"He's out tomorrow morning," I said.

"And me too, I suppose," Megan asked.

"Yes," Claudia replied. "Sorry."

The next afternoon when I got home from work, they were gone. Our living room was back to normal–though it still smelled of Dirk. I sighed, chuckling with joy at having the apartment to ourselves again.

Dirk had left a pencil sketch on the table. It was a view of the street from our window. The guy was no artist, but perhaps he could make some money drawing for tourists in the Place du Tertre.

"You want this?" I asked Claudia.

She laughed. "Are you kidding?"

I dropped the sketch into the trash basket and brushed my hands. "Ahhh," I sighed. "How about some wine to celebrate?"

"I'll get the glasses," she said.

I selected a bottle of Beaujolais and was reaching for my Laguiole wine opener when the buzzer sounded.

"Oh, please," Claudia muttered.

I wasn't in the mood to run downstairs, afraid it might be Dirk again, so I opened the window. Two figures stood on the sidewalk. When I called out, one of them gazed up at me. He had a round face with a scraggly beard and a bowl haircut like a medieval serf. It was our Dutch friend Wim from Africa. I couldn't believe it.

"Wim!" I shouted.

"*Hallo,*" he called.

"Come up!"

We hadn't seen him since we left Pindjali. In those days he was living with an adorable redhead named Turnje. We had shared many experiences together–most of them humorous. Wim's life seemed to be one catastrophe after another–including driving off a washed-out bridge, accidentally burning down his house while filling a lantern, and his windshield breaking out during a sandstorm in the Sahara Desert. We never knew what to expect when he arrived, but he was an entertaining friend and we loved his visits.

"This is Everett," he said, introducing us to his companion.

Everett grinned broadly. He had a tanned face with dark hair and dark eyebrows. I imagined his ancestors might have come from Spain or perhaps from one of the central European countries. He held out his hand with difficulty because he was carrying a case of beer.

Wim held another case.

"We like our beer," Wim said.

"I remember," I said.

"We each drink about a case a day," Everett said.

"Well then," I said, laughing. "Let the party begin."

When we got upstairs, Claudia saw the cases of beer and put away the wine glasses. She hugged Wim, and we settled in for a visit.

Wim told us he and Turnje had split up for the time being, and that another Dutch couple we had known in Africa were divorced. This was sad news, but expected. Even in Pindjali, their lives seemed to be going in different directions.

The next morning while Claudia and I worked, Wim and Everett visited Montmartre, Place St.-Michel, and the Pompidou Center. In the evening, we were invited to a friend's apartment for dinner. Andrea De Luna was Italian, though she had spent time in the states and spoke English very well. She was dark and trim and a talented water-color artist. She shared the apartment with her brother, Matteo, who had more running shoes than anyone I'd ever met. A row of at least twenty new pairs lined his bedroom wall. He showed them to us with pride.

Andrea's apartment was on the fifth floor of her building. I had called ahead and asked if we could bring our Dutch friends. She had said yes, so the four of us were now standing in front of a small lift on the ground floor.

"There's only room for three," Claudia said, gazing at the narrow compartment.

"That's okay," I said. "You three go. I'll take the stairs."

"You're sure?" she asked.

"No problem."

After my experience in Africa of being roped to a table for appendicitis surgery, I wasn't going to wedge myself into a tight elevator. Also, I hadn't worked out for a few days and needed the exercise.

"I'll race you to the top," I said and took off up the stairs.

When I got to the top, they were still in the lift and talking excitedly. Claudia's voice was on the verge of panic.

I opened the lift door and saw the three of them crunched together, looking in the wrong direction. They thought the lift opening was on the other side. I barely suppressed a laugh.

"How do we get out of here?" Claudia asked, panicked.

"The latch must be around here somewhere," Wim said.

I was standing behind them with the lift door open. They were feeling around on the far wall.

"Why don't you just turn around and come out?" I asked quietly.

The three of them froze. Then they turned and saw me standing there. We all burst into laughter.

The next evening, we accompanied Wim and Everett to Pigalle in search of an authentic West African restaurant. Since we were with our African friend, we wanted to savor the moment by eating peanut sauce and pounded yams. We strolled around the rue de Clignancourt for a while until Wim began asking pedestrians for any African restaurants in the quarter. A young man finally told us about a place near the Métro Chauteau Rouge.

"This restaurant does not have pounded yams," he said. "But it does have peanut sauce and rice. Very good."

"Wonderful," Claudia exclaimed.

"If you like," he offered. "I will take you."

We accepted eagerly.

When we arrived at the little restaurant, our guide paused at the door.

"*C'est ici,*" he said.

He had the round face and broad cheekbones of a Dioula. Possibly he was from West Africa.

"Would you like to eat with us?" I asked.

"*Moi?*" he asked.

"Yes."

His serious expression transformed into a broad grin, and he nodded happily.

"What's your name?" Claudia asked him, as we entered the restaurant.

"Sako," he replied.

Her mouth dropped.

Sako was the name of the Dioula student who had lived with us in Pindjali.

A young woman waited on us. She spoke Dioula, and Everett fell in love with her immediately. She brought us large bowls of rice and peanut sauce—known in French as *sauce arachide*—that contained hunks of fish. *Do You Feel My Love* by Eddie Grant was booming from an overhead speaker. Claudia ordered a glass of *Gnamakoudji*—a juice drink prepared from ginger root sugar and water. We had missed living in the Ivory Coast and this brought it all back. We had a wonderful time and the food was delicious.

When we returned to our apartment later that evening, Hailey knocked on our door and invited us to a party.

"Bring your beer," she said.

She knew how much our Dutch friends liked to drink.

At the party we nibbled on cheese and olives, and supplemented the beer with shots of vodka. By one o'clock in the morning, the beer was gone and I was tired. I had to work the next morning. But Wim, Everett, and Claudia were only getting started. Taking a taxi to an all-might store near the Centre Pompidou, they bought more beer.

At one thirty, they climbed the stairs to our apartment where I was trying to sleep and continued to drink and sing. Claudia came to the bedroom doorway, gazed at me in the bed, and shook her head sadly.

"Every party has a pooper, that's why we invited you," she sang. "Party pooper!"

"We'll see how you feel about that in the morning," I muttered and put a pillow over my head.

Wim and Everett caught a train to Amsterdam the next morning. I didn't get to see them off, as I was already at work. I had tip-toed past their unconscious bodies at six thirty. However, I was able to reach them by phone.

"We will see each other again … somewhere," Wim said.

That afternoon Claudia was pale and shaking.

"My head feels like someone put it in a micro-wave," she groaned. "And my eyes feel rusty."

"You were unstoppable," I said.

"We had so much fun at the African restaurant and then I started drinking Hailey's vodka."

She massaged her temples.

"Vodka can be deadly," I offered. "Especially after so much beer."

"Oh, the beer," she gulped and looked as if she might be sick.

"I have an idea," I said. "Let's call Pindjali and talk with Marty and Martha. That will make you feel better."

Marty and Martha were missionaries we had known in Pindjali. They had recently installed a telephone in their mission house.

"Okay," she said, and I dialed the number.

We had a pleasant chat with our old friends and then I got out the wine and cork screw.

"Time for that drink," I said.

"To celebrate us being alone?" she asked.

"Exactly."

I opened the wine and filled our glasses. I handed one to Claudia.

"To alone time," I said.

We clinked glasses and were raising the wine to our lips when the door buzzer sounded.

"If that's another visitor, I'm going to kill myself," Claudia said, closing her eyes and resting her forehead on her palm.

I looked out the window.

"You wanna dive out the window, or stick your head in the oven like Sylvia Plath?"

"Don't joke with me," she said.

"I'm not."

"You mean ... there's someone down there?"

I nodded.

"Who?"

"Wilke."

"Mike is here? Oh, my Gosh!"

Claudia jumped up. Mike was one of her oldest friends. German by heritage, he had grown up in Minnesota. In addition to many other things, he was a world-traveler, carpenter, counselor, serious cyclist, and free spirit.

"Well," I said, glancing at my watch. "We got ... hmm ... twenty minutes."

Claudia ignored this.

"We can't leave him standing down there," she said. "Let him in and I'll straighten up the place."

Mike was the most amiable of guys. He was quiet and modest, with an easy smile. He had strong views on life and people, and I always found him interesting.

Claudia had been trying for weeks to get tickets to a jazz performance by Claude Bolling. He was one of our favorite pianists. We loved his album *Suite for Flute and Jazz Piano* with Jean Pierre Rampal.

When I got home the next afternoon, she and Mike were holding tickets.

"You got them?" I asked.

"Yes," Claudia replied, beaming. "Mike helped. They're for tonight. Isn't it wonderful?"

"Amazing," I said.

Bolling was playing at a dimly lit club in the Latin Quarter. As we were shown to our table, we passed a small stage with his piano, the drums, and a bass guitar already set up. The room was so hazy with cigarette smoke I could hardly see.

A brick support column blocked our view of the stage. From our table, we could hear Bolling *play* perfectly well – he was only ten feet away-but we couldn't *see* him. With the low ceiling, smoky haze, and press of the crowd, I was content to relax, sip my beer, and listen to the music. Claudia, however, wanted to see and leaned her chair almost to the tipping point to watch.

"I like Zydeco music," Mike said. "Boozoo Chavis rocks."

"He does," I said, coughing in the smoke.

Claude Bolling came onstage. Claudia closed her eyes dreamily and swayed in her chair as the jazz notes rose from his piano. The performance lasted nearly an hour and a half. It would have been fun to see.

The next morning, Claudia took Mike on a tour of our favorite places in Paris while I had my classes. We met up for dinner in the Latin Quarter. Then it was time for him to catch his train to London.

It was oddly quiet when we returned to our apartment.

"Wine?" I asked.

"To celebrate?" she replied.

I nodded.

For some reason, the excitement of being alone this time wasn't the same. We had passed several weeks of busy social activity with friends and strangers and now our apartment felt small, confined, lonely.

I began to fill Claudia's wine glass when she held out a hand to stop me.

"Let's go down to the café and drink a glass of wine there," she suggested.

"Great idea," I said. "And then we can walk up to the Place du Republique."

"We haven't done that for a while," she said, laughing.

The evening was brightening already.

The door buzzer sounded.

"You're kidding," Claudia muttered.

I pushed the button and we heard footsteps coming up the stairs. I opened the door and waited.

Soon a tall figure carrying a heavy duffle approached the landing.

It was Wilke.

"I missed my train," he said. "May I come in?"

Chapter 26
Departures & Arrivals

Étretat is a beautiful seaside town in Normandy. It is known for the Porte d'Aval-a slender arch attached to the white chalk cliffs, and L'Aiguille–a natural stone pillar that rises from the sea near the arch. Monet painted both, and I was eager to see the town and coastline for myself. Claudia loved Normandy for its seafood (especially mussels and scallops), *Canard àla Rouennaise* (a tasty duck dish) and cheeses such as *Camembert* and *Pont-l'Evêque.*

When Hailey Barrow told us she was driving to Étretat for the weekend and asked if we'd like to go, we accepted immediately. It would be refreshing to leave Paris for a few days. It was May now and the cold snap that had blown across France seemed to be the last gasp of winter. People were opening their windows and planting colorful flowers in their flower boxes. Girls on the streets were wearing the latest Paris fashions: short skirts, blouses with snaps, and all in aqua green or candy pink colors. I had also read that the weather over the channel was bright with scattered clouds, so it seemed like a perfect time to go.

Hailey had made reservations at a Bed & Breakfast in Étretat, so we called and added a room for ourselves. The only drawback was that we were once again riding with Hailey behind the wheel. I hoped we would make it and gripped my knees as we shot up the Boulevard Voltaire.

The B&B in Étretat was a large three-story house on the edge of town. It was made of stone and mortar with a brick trim and a gray slate roof. Upon our arrival, a thin, white-haired woman of perhaps seventy greeted us at the door. A plaid wool shawl around her shoulders made her look more Scottish than French. Madame D'Abernon welcomed us inside and gave us a brief tour. The main floor hallway led to a large front room with a grand piano and a dining room with wooden tables.

"You see the tiles?" she asked as we passed up the hallway.

Small white tiles covered the hallway with French-blue tiles around the edges. The tiles were badly scuffed. I assumed this was from the passage of so many guests over the years.

"Not from guests," Madame D'Abernon said, wagging a finger. "From the Germans ... their hob-nail boots. Always walking up and down." She made a motion with her fingers. "Ruined my floor."

I studied the scuff marks more closely. We were staying in a house the Germans had occupied during World War II. It brought the conflict much closer and added a sense of realism I had never felt before.

Our rooms were on the third floor. Claudia and I were given a corner room. Hailey's room was farther down the hallway. As we passed one door, Madame D'Abernon hesitated and smiled.

"This was Winston Churchill's room," she said, with a twinkle in her eye. "He sometimes came here in the summers to paint. Did you know he was an artist?"

I shook my head. "No."

"Yes," she said. "One of his paintings is downstairs."

"Can we see the room?" I asked.

She gave a little shrug and pursed her lips. "Perhaps tomorrow."

The next day it was raining. A storm front had blown across the channel, bringing with it overcast skies and drizzling rain. Nothing like the weather report I had read. We slept late, buried under thick warm blankets. When we finally got up, Claudia started her yoga exercises while I dressed and pulled on a warm sweater.

Downstairs, four people sat around one of the tables: Hailey, a Belgian business executive, and a young couple from Zagreb. The young man was an architect. We shared a relaxed breakfast, drinking coffee and tea and eating fresh baguettes with butter, jam, or pate.

Afterwards, I wandered into the front room and sat at the grand piano. The room was facing the channel and was drafty, so that my fingers were cold on the keys. I spied a small blanket draped over the sofa and put this around my shoulders.

Hailey stepped into the room and paused with an amused expression on her face. She listened to me playing for a minute.

"You look like one of those old-time composers," she said, laughing. "Like Chopin or Schumann."

"I wish," I said.

Claudia came into the room.

"We're going to the market," she announced. "Want to go?"

"Thanks," I replied. "But I've got the new book to read."

I had recently purchased a copy of *Gandhi: A Memoir* by William Shirer. I imagined spending the day seated on the bank of the Ganges with Gandhi in my homespun clothes. Also, it felt good to stay warm in the old house with the damp wind gusting outside.

I had only gotten as far as chapter two, however, when I heard the rush of footsteps in the hallway.

"Hailey is leaving," Claudia said, coming into the room. "She just got word her father died."

Hailey had talked a lot about her parents, and I knew she was close to her father. This was devastating news.

"She wants to leave in an hour," Claudia continued. "Is that okay?"

"Sure," I said. "But I wanna do something before we go."

"What?"

"See Churchill's room."

Madame D'Abernon unlocked the door and pushed it open. The bedroom was similar to ours, except that its windows opened onto a beautiful view of the town and the cliffs beyond. This was an artist's view. Also, the light was good and I could imagine Churchill seated in front of his canvas, paintbrush in hand, and gazing out the window as he painted. It was ironic that the British Prime Minister had used a house once occupied by the Wehrmacht as a refuge to rest and paint.

We made the return trip to Paris with me driving. Hailey sat hunched in the backseat as we rolled through the Normandy countryside. I didn't realize it, but this was our last encounter with her. She not only left Étretat, but decided to leave Paris all together and return to Seattle. We were sorry to see her go.

Friendships you make in foreign countries are at once more intense and yet more fleeting than friendships you make at home. The relationships are more intense because you spend more time together, depend on each other more, and share the common bond of living in a foreign location. Yet they are more fleeting because in most cases when the friend leaves the place in which you have known them: France, Italy, England, Africa, etc., you seldom see them again. They—and you—are off to new adventures and friendships.

It was sad to pass Hailey's door and know she would no longer greet us with her bright smile, her eager advice on living in Paris, and invitations to her zany parties. Vacant apartments are quickly snapped up, and only a few days later a young man and woman were outside our building. The young woman was holding open the heavy door while the young man struggled with an enormous television set. He was lean with curly black hair, intense dark eyes, and an aquiline nose. He had the look of a long-distance runner. The young woman was blonde and sweetly appealing.

"Can I help?" I asked.

"Thanks, but I got it," he said.

"Are you moving into the second-floor apartment?"

This wasn't a Sherlock Holmes quality deduction. Hailey's was the only vacant apartment in the building.

"That's right," he replied, gripping the TV. "And you?"

"We live on the third floor." I started to hold out my hand, but his were occupied.

"I'm Bobby," he said. "This is Molly."

He flashed a quick, eager grin. She gazed at me shyly.

"I just bought this TV for 300 francs," he said.

"Hope it works," I said.

He grinned. "Me too."

Seeing Bobby standing there with the TV in his hands reminded me of an incident that had happened only a few weeks earlier. Theft was common in our neighborhood and I was always careful about checking the door lock when I left for work. However, it didn't really matter if you had one lock or a dozen–the thieves used crowbars to splinter the door frames and get inside.

Claudia and her friend Bea were chatting outside our building one afternoon when two men came running down the street carrying a large television. Claudia and Bea watched the men race up to a car, pop the trunk, and shove the TV set inside.

"My," Claudia said, laughing. "They're certainly in a hurry to watch the soccer game!"

It was only when one of the men tossed a crowbar into the trunk that she realized the situation.

"I think they just stole that TV," she mused.

"I think you're right," Bea said.

Neither of them got the license plate number of the car.

"Really?" I asked, when she told me the story. "That's what you were thinking? They were in a hurry to watch the game?"

"You know guys," Claudia said. "They love sports."

Bobby moved into Hailey's apartment and we got to know each other. He was from Toronto and worked as assistant editor for Paris Passion Magazine, a journal founded by Robert Sarner. As we discussed journalism and writing in general, I felt a rapport with him that I'd never felt with Rob Parsons of the Paris Free Voice.

"We do more work with journalists who are simple writers but get the job done, than we do with brilliant but erratic types," he told me once about the magazine. "Persistence is the key. Just keep slugging away."

Claudia was soon inviting Bobby and Molly up for dinner.

One evening they were late and when they finally arrived, they looked exhausted.

"We just watched a four-and-a-half-hour version of Richard II performed Kabuki Style," Bobby said.

"Have a beer," I said.

Bobby knew I'd written for the Paris Free Voice and asked if I'd be interested in writing an article on Monet's house in Giverny. When I turned it in, he gave me a choice.

"I can either pay you, or offer you two tickets to a Marcel Marceau performance," he said. "Which would you prefer?"

Marcel Marceau was the most famous mime artist in the world.

"Are you kidding?" I asked. "We'd love to see him."

Mimes frequently performed on the streets in Paris and outside the Centre Pompidou, but this was the master and we were excited.

The performance was at the Theatre Champs-Élysées. I met Claudia after her refugee class. We ate dinner at a nearby restaurant and then headed to the theatre. When the usher escorted us to our seats, we discovered we were in the front row center. This was fantastic. My feet could touch the stage.

The curtains parted and Marcel Marceau took the stage dressed as Bip the Clown.

The rest ... as they say ...

... was silence.

Chapter 27
The Lost Years

I gazed with mild surprise at the bowl of gooey bread-dough balls in front of me. Please don't let this be dinner.

Peter and Tanya had invited Claudia, Glen, Catherine, and I to their apartment for dinner. They lived in Arcueil-Cachan, a suburb of Paris, and it was a long ride by Métro and RER. By the time I arrived from school, I was hungry and thirsty for a cold drink.

Claudia blew me a kiss from the table. She had come directly from her class at Montmorency. Glen and Catherine sat beside her.

I was excited because Tanya was an excellent cook. Only a few weeks earlier, she had invited us to a delicious dinner of Czech liver dumpling soup. The dumplings consisted of ground calf's liver, egg, garlic, salt and pepper, and breadcrumbs, and cooked in a tasty broth. I thought it was the best soup I'd ever tasted. Pan-fried pork steaks and potatoes followed this, with a strawberry charlotte for dessert. And of course, it was all washed down with a great quantity of beer.

Now I was gazing at these buttery-slick balls of dough. Was this a Czech delicacy?

"What is it?" Catherine asked, pushing at a ball with her fork.

"Czech fruit dumplings," Tanya replied. "Each ball has half an apricot inside. You wrap the apricot in bread dough and drop it into boiling water. Next, you sprinkle on powdered sugar and pour melted butter over it."

"Sounds very rich," Claudia remarked.

"We're having dessert first!" Glen exclaimed happily.

"This is a special dinner," Tanya said, smiling shyly and brushing the dark bangs from her eyes. "We have news."

"You have a departure date for Canada?" I asked.

At the Canadian embassy, they were told they would depart for Winnipeg in three or four months. It had almost been three months now.

"Even more important," Tanya replied, taking Peter's hand. "We're getting married."

It was obvious they loved each other and had been through an extraordinary ordeal in getting across the border to freedom. We all assumed they would get married someday, but didn't know when the ceremony might happen.

"Next month," Peter announced. "You are all invited. We hope you can come."

"Of course," we said, raising our glasses. "Congratulations!"

We clinked glasses.

"Now to dinner," Tanya said.

"One more toast," I said, holding out my glass.

We toasted several more times before any of us were ready to try the boiled dumplings.

The weeks passed quickly with preparations for the wedding. Peter and Tanya wanted to get married at the Meudon Town Hall. A reception would be held at an old stone house overlooking Paris. Invitations went out to friends in Paris, London, and the south of France.

"My father is coming," Peter informed me.

"I'm looking forward to meeting him," I said.

I'd heard so many stories about Marek Bressler: how he had attended a secret political discussion group that favored democracy, how he was performing with the Prague Symphony in London when Russian tanks rolled into Czechoslovakia, how he was warned not to return to Prague because he would be arrested as a dissident, how he had taken refuge in France and now had a girlfriend and lived in Provence.

We finally met at a pre-wedding party given by Glen and Catherine. Marek was a heavy-set man with slicked brassy hair, jowls, and the sagging eyelids and red-tinged complexion of a heavy drinker. Add to this the yellow-stained nails on the thumb and first finger of a frequent smoker.

"I have heard about you from Peter," he said. "Thank you for helping them."

"My pleasure," I said. "They're remarkable."

Peter and Tanya *were* remarkable. I admired their courage, tenacity, and love of music. I envied their determination to make a better life for themselves.

"Yes," he said and took a sip of scotch. "They wanted so much to live in the United States."

"I know," I said, still feeling guilty and embarrassed by their rejection.

"But they will be happy in Canada," he added.

"I think so too," I said. "I love Canada. My grandfather was Canadian."

Marek gazed at me with his blood-shot eyes.

"You westerners have no idea what life is like in a communist country," he said. "The difficulties ... paranoia ... depression ... bleakness."

"I've read about it," I replied. "But I know that's not the same."

"It's a gray life with no hope," Marek continued. "That is the worst part. When there is no hope for the future, what's the point?"

"You escape," Peter offered, coming over to us.

"Yes, yes," his father said.

Peter picked up his guitar. Marek removed his violin from the case, tuned it, and held it to his shoulder. From the rapturous expressions on their faces as they played, you could truly see they were father and son. Afterwards, we talked about Marek's defection and how circumstances had forced him to leave his wife and two sons in Prague.

"Twelve years," he grumbled, swirling the scotch in his glass. "They kept me from my family for twelve years." He glanced at Peter. "Then I see this young man at the station ... no longer my ten-year-old boy."

Tears came to his eyes.

"We lost so much," Peter muttered.

On their wedding day, Tanya looked beautiful in a white dress. Peter wore a tailored grey suit. The Mayor of Meudon performed the ceremony, and then we went to the reception.

As I watched Marek dancing with his new daughter-in-law, I thought about life and how world events like the Prague Spring could spread far beyond government strife to affect the lives of individual people; even the life of a classical violinist who wished only to play Dvorak and watch his youngest son grow up.

I also wondered if Marek had eaten Tanya's Czech fruit dumplings.

Now there was true love.

Chapter 28
Jogging with Hemingway

"Ready?' Bobby asked, tightening the laces on his running shoes.

"Lead on MacDuff," I said, laughing. (The correct line from MacBeth is 'Lay on MacDuff', but it didn't seem to fit here since we weren't talking about sword fighting.)

Bobby took off along the Boulevard du Temple and I fell in beside him. It was a beautiful Sunday afternoon, a spring day in Paris, the kind you think of when you've left France and remember living there. As you lay huddled under blankets in some faraway country, your mind conjures up images of colorful Parisian cafes, broad sunny boulevards, parks alive with daffodils and tulips, and fashionable women in tight skirts strolling up the Rue Royale. It is a trick of the mind that you quickly forget the overcast skies, rain, and chilly wind that so often represent life in Paris.

The afternoon light threw the poplar trees and apartment buildings along the boulevard into bright contrast. There was only a minimum of weekend traffic to blow exhaust fumes into our faces. If only it could be this way all the time, I thought, as my Nike shoes-seemingly equipped with built-in detectors-hopped nimbly over a pile of dog poop on the sidewalk.

We ran down to the Bastille with its tall green Colonne de Juillet monument rising from the cobblestones, and then along the canal on the Boulevard Bourdon to the Pont D'Austerlitz. The Quai Saint Bernard was peaceful as we jogged toward Notre Dame Cathedral.

This was a typical weekend run for us and we usually spent our time talking about writing—which inevitably brought us to Hemingway. We talked about his early stories, his life in Paris, his adventures, and the bars, cafes, and restaurants he had frequented. Many of them we had visited ourselves.

"Maybe he would've run with us," Bobby suggested.

"With his bad leg?" I asked.

"He rode bicycles and played tennis."

I tried to imagine the heavy-set writer with his war-scarred legs trying to keep up with Bobby, who was built lean and small like a long-distance runner. Hemingway worked out on the roads like a boxer, but this kind of running was different. I also wondered what we would talk about if he were with us now. It wouldn't be writing–unless he was discussing someone else's work. He would probably want to talk about horse racing, boxing, or bullfights. That's of course if he could breathe, trying to keep pace with Bobby.

I laughed, thinking about this.

"What's so funny?" Bobby asked.

"I was trying to imagine what Hemingway would talk about if he was running with us."

"Long story short," Bobby said, and grinned. "Himself."

"You think so?" I asked.

"No," he said. "It's spring. Maybe baseball."

Bobby was from Toronto and a Blue Jays fan.

We reached the Pont de Sully and cut back across the Seine, skirting the edge of the Île Saint-Louis with its picturesque quay lined by the heavy stone wall–now stained in places by high water–and the stately old houses with their slate-gray roofs. This was my favorite part of the run, crossing the Pont de Sully with the Notre Dame Cathedral on our left. If I could have afforded to live anywhere in Paris, it would've been on the Île Saint-Louis–as did James Jones, author of *From Here to Eternity*. Claudia would have lived there for Berthillon, the famous sorbet shop.

Working our way over to the Place des Vosges, Bobby and I leaned into the rue de Turenne and kicked it out on the long straightaway toward the rue de Malte.

A few weeks later, a friend invited Claudia and me to run with his cross-country club. This was a mixture of mostly French and a few American runners who met every weekend and ran for several hours through the backstreets of Paris–finishing at a café.

"Would you like to go?" I asked her.

We frequently went on walks around the city or the Parc des Buttes Chaumont, but she didn't run that often.

"I'd like to try," she said.

So, with muscles warmed up and stretched to their maximum potential, we joined our friend the next Sunday morning at the Parc de Monceau. There were about fifteen runners in the group. With them all moving around, it was difficult to count.

Unfortunately, Claudia and I had made the *faux pas* of being dressed in old tee shirts and athletic shorts. We considered this a workout. The French, on the other hand, were dressed in colorful running costumes as if they were in the Olympics.

I had noticed this trait before. Comparable to the Italians, the French took pride in dressing the part for any athletic activity in which they participated. If they were riding bicycles, they looked like Tour de France riders. As runners, they were all attired to break the tape and win the gold medal at the end of the course. We, by contract, were lowly American joggers–not *sportifs*-and certainly not *sportifs* with all the accessories.

We'd been running about thirty minutes when Claudia skipped over to the curb.

"It's my shoe," she said.

Pulling off the offending shoe, she gave it a hearty shake. A small, black peddle fell out.

"Ah," she sighed, lacing her shoe back on. "It was driving me crazy."

We had just topped the Place du Sacre Coeur with the iconic white church rising above our heads. Ahead lay a maze of narrow lanes and older apartments vintage early Picasso. The running group had gone straight ahead. We weren't far behind. I felt confident we could catch up within a few minutes.

"Are you ready?" I asked.

Claudia nodded and held out a hand for me to pull her up.

"Which way did they go?" she asked.

"Straight ahead."

She scanned the hill. "I don't see them."

"They can't be far."

We took off running.

We ran this way and that way, cutting to the left and right, always hopeful, and not quite believing that we'd lost a group of fifteen runners. How was this possible? We'd only stopped for a moment.

A certain herd mentality keeps you going when you're running in a group. Perhaps it's simply that you're shielded from the wind, but you aren't as aware of the energy you're expending or the steepness of the terrain. Away from the group and running on your own, you suddenly feel every stride and swing of the arms. What seemed before like gliding is now slogging; where you once felt like a cougar, now you're a hippo. The difference is amazing. No longer shielded by the herd, you're acutely aware of your position in the open as a solitary runner. It isn't a pleasant feeling.

After about ten minutes, Claudia halted and stood with hands on her hips, catching her breath.

"This is ridiculous," she gasped. "Where'd they go?"

"No idea," I said. "They could be miles away by now."

She looked at me. "I've had enough. Let's get something to drink."

We tried running back up the hill to the Place du Sacre Coeur, but after a few blocks, Claudia stopped.

"Forget it," she huffed. "I'm walking."

At the Place du Tertre, we seated ourselves at a café table and sighed with audible relief. This was life in Paris as it should be–not gallivanting around the narrow lanes like a herd of caffeinated goats. Here we could quietly sip a cold beer and study the tourists who sat for their portraits. Down the hill and around the corner was Picasso's old studio, where he had invented cubism with the friendly competition of Georges Braque.

I gazed at Claudia. Her cheeks were red from the exertion and she sipped contentedly at her glass of chilled white wine.

"Well," she said, brushing damp hair from her face. "What now?"

"I was thinking maybe a game of squash," I suggested.

"But of course," she replied with a fakey-French accent. "Right after I climb ze Eiffel Tower."

"From the outside?"

"Bien sûr, Monsieur."

"Nice rhyming," I said.

I thought of Hemingway sitting in the Brasserie Lipp with its starched white tablecloths, ornate mirrored walls accented by yellow and blue tiles, and wondered if he'd ever played squash or jogged around Montmartre. And what would he talk about if he were here now–not back in the 1920s, but here now? Would his subjects of discourse change? I imagined they would. The work of popular artists, writers, or musicians is woven into the fabric of the era in which they live. Take them out of that era, and their life and work would naturally be different; perhaps not as meaningful.

"C'mon," Claudia said. "Let's go home and have lunch."

Now we were talking.

And next Sunday Bobby and I would run again and talk more about Hemingway, as there was always something more to say and to learn and to understand.

Chapter 29
Montmartre Life

We enjoyed visiting Montmartre in the pleasant weather. The narrow streets and Place du Tertre with its old cafes and portrait artists (though hopelessly touristic) reminded me of La Belle Époque. On Sundays, we relaxed on the broad steps of the Sacre Coeur and admired the view of the city. We also appreciated the quiet sanctity of the chapel's interior. But we had never visited anyone who lived in Montmartre, until one of the Paris Free Voice staff writers invited us to a party.

Abby wrote feature articles on women's issues, so I hadn't worked with her directly, but I saw her at staff meetings and a group of us had gone out for lunch. She often wore a pink tee shirt, blue-jean overalls, and red high-top Converse tennis shoes. She was quiet and shy with a calm smile and natural laugh. I'd heard she was from London, but didn't know which part.

"Most of the staff will be there," she said. "Rob is coming if his girlfriend isn't performing."

Rob's girlfriend was a dancer in the Paris Ballet.

"Where do you live?" I asked.

"On the rue Lepic," Abby replied. "You can't miss it. Look for the blondes."

Blondes? I thought, as we passed the building where Theo Van Gogh had lived. When we reached the Rue Lepic, I saw what Abby meant. A group of transvestites dressed in blonde wigs stood on the street corner.

"Darn," Claudia muttered. "I forgot my wig."

"Me too," I said.

The two-story frame structure had a narrow walkway to the street. An old-fashioned elegance transformed it into a writer's flat, a poet's bungalow, secluded and yet in the midst of everything-the swirl of art life, street life, and the city itself.

In the front room, mingled an assortment of exotically dressed guests. Indian sitar music floated from a speaker. I considered leaving when we saw Abby across the room. She greeted us warmly and introduced us to Kate, an English woman in her early thirties who owned the apartment. Kate's daughter Charlotte was an adorable three-year-old.

"Eat something and go to bed," Kate told the little girl.

"Yes, Mama," Charlotte replied and flitted off.

Someone had painted a daffodil on Charlotte's cheek, which blended nicely with her honey-golden hair. I couldn't imagine raising a child in such an environment—or trying to sleep.

As the evening progressed, we learned that Kate was Den Mother to a flotsam of British misfits who had washed up against her door. She had five tenants in all: Rico, Gavin, Maggie, Jayne, and Abby. Perhaps it was her wire-rimmed glasses or the way she folded her arms and tilted her head amusedly as someone was talking, but Kate emitted a maternal quality. I imagined it was this quality that had attracted people who needed structure or boundaries in their lives.

The first tenant I got to know was Gavin, a husky young man who looked like a rugby player but wanted to be an artist. His canvases covered the walls of his room and were stacked in the corners. He had taken to pasting things onto his paintings and you were never sure what you might find adorning one of his newly finished canvases—a newspaper clipping from Le Figaro, a lid from a jar of marmalade, a pigeon feather, a burnt match, a Métro ticket.

Sometimes he would take a pile of oddities he had collected, put them in a burlap sack, and bury them in a grassy strip near the Cimetière Montmartre. A month later, he would dig them up and apply the now earthy pieces to his canvas. He spliced them together with squares of hastily applied acrylic paint.

Gavin and I got to be friends and we often visited the local cafés. I'd never known a guy who could drink eight whiskey sodas in one evening. For me, this was remarkable even by college standards. My best was six and then I had a terrible hangover the next morning and promised myself never to do it again.

"I'm tormented by my dreams," Gavin confided to me one evening, turning the crystal edges of his whiskey glass against the red and blue café bar lights. "I drink to keep them away."

"Can't be very productive," I said.

"You'd be surprised," he said and grinned.

Gavin had a shy girlfriend in Maggie, a waif-like young woman who wanted to be a magazine editor. She must have loved him unconditionally to spend time in the studio with its toxic fumes of paint and thinner. Sometimes when they staggered into the kitchen, I would gaze at their pallid faces and wonder how they survived.

I never got to know Jayne very well. She was about the same age as Kate and had worked in a Notting Hill book shop before a divorce had left her in emotional shambles. She was always friendly to us, yet reserved. I had the impression she was desperately holding onto herself, as one might with the cracked pieces of a Chinese vase.

One afternoon I found Jayne seated on a floral couch in the parlor. She sat there alone, rocking slowly back and forth, her arms wrapped around herself. It was a gray afternoon and the pale light seemed to suit her mood.

"Are you alright?" I asked.

She gazed at me. Her dark green eyes searched mine and I felt she was trying to decide if she could trust me. The way she was holding herself seemed protective.

"You know me," she said. "My past."

"A bit," I replied.

She gave a shiver. "I went down to Place Pigalle last night. I needed to be around people."

"Uh huh."

"I met a guy."

"That's good," I said.

"No," she said and rocked again. "Not good. We went back to his flat and he pulled a knife on me."

"What?"

"He wanted to cut my throat." She touched a trembling fingertip to the pale skin above her jugular.

I saw dried blood.

"Have you contacted the gendarmes?"

She nodded. "I spent all night talking to him, trying to calm him down, trying to understand. Hoping he wouldn't ..."

She began to shake all over, her thin shoulders trembling.

"I can't breathe," she gasped. "It was so close ... *so* close."

"Can I get you anything?"

She smiled. "A new life?"

I thought for a moment. "Would it help to talk with Claudia? She's been through this."

"It happened to her?" Jayne asked.

"To a friend."

"Thanks," she said. "But I'd rather not think about it."

***

Claudia and I spent the following summer in Switzerland. When we returned to Paris after a beautiful vacation in Tuscany, our lives spun in another direction. We didn't get around to visiting Kate's apartment again, and I was no longer writing for the Free Voice, which meant I didn't see Abby. So, it shocked me when I ran into her one afternoon near the Gare St. Lazare. Her appearance had transformed. Gone were the blue jean overalls, pink tee shirt, and Converse tennis shoes. Now she wore a tailored beige suit with stockings and pumps. Her dark-brown hair was dyed a subtle reddish color. She was thinner, but not in a healthy way. She looked ten years older.

"I'm so glad to see you," she said, giving me a hug. "Can we talk for a minute?"

Her warm greeting surprised me. We had worked together on the Free Voice and she had invited us to Kate's apartment for the staff party, but I'd never gotten the impression she thought of me as a close friend. Perhaps any friend would do now.

"Okay," I said, glancing at my watch.

We found a table at a nearby café and she told me about her relationship with a French executive. He was fifteen years older, she said, and wealthy. This was a man who could whisk her away to Spain for a weekend or buy her expensive jewelry.

After telling me this, Abby gazed at me intently. She looked as if she might start crying. I understood now why she was pleased to see me. I was a friend from the old days. Apparently, she had been happier then, living the life of an expatriate journalist in Paris.

A tear rolled down her rouged cheek.

"I have a thirteen-year-old daughter," she said abruptly. "Thirteen! And here I was-living in Paris like a bloody thirteen-year-old myself!"

"Time to grow up?" I asked.

She nodded. "Though I can't say I'm happy."

"You don't look it," I said.

Abby picked up a napkin and dabbed her cheeks. "I'd like to see her again. She's in Hampstead with my parents."

"How long has it been?" I asked.

"Two years."

"How's your relationship?"

"Good when I see her." Abby hesitated and stared at me. "I can imagine what you're thinking. What a mother, right?" She gave a tearful laugh. "I was sixteen when I had her. Practically a child myself, you know. Not mature enough to be a mum yet. And now ..."

"You want to see her," I said.

Abby waved a hand toward herself. "Look at me. This isn't *me*. I'm not some bloody French business woman. This isn't my life!"

"What about the trips to Spain?" I asked.

She emitted a sad chuckle and shook her head. "How many times can you go? Even Spain gets old after a while."

"What about the French guy?"

Abby wiped her cheeks again, made a face, and shrugged.

"I have to talk with him," she said. "It's going to be a long evening."

Grabbing her handbag, she gave me a quick kiss on the cheek.

"Good to see you again," she said.

Then she turned and hurried into the crowd on the sidewalk.

Just like that, I thought. A chance encounter, a confession, and gone. I felt like I should have asked her to say ten Hail Marys.

***

I have fond memories of the friendships I made in Montmartre: discussing art with Gavin, shaking my head at Kate's den-mother qualities, Charlotte with her painted cheeks, Jayne's perilously close call with a knife blade, and Abby sailing back to England to begin a new life with her daughter. Those were interesting moments. However, when a road closes behind you, there is no alternative but to press on. And as way leads on to way …

We can only hope the next experience will be just as rewarding.

This was life in Montmartre.

Chapter 30
Yesterday and Today

Paris is the city of light and life, but on nearly every street corner you are reminded of those who came before you. Of the writers, poets, artists, musicians, politicians, religious leaders, and French resistance fighters who lived and died among these cobble-stone streets, tall old buildings, gardens, boulevards, islands, and banks of the Seine. It is not only in the Cimetiere du Pere Lachaise or the Cimetiere du Montparnasse, but in the buildings themselves–rising like rain-dampened tombstones from the various quarters. How many people remembered Madame de Brinvilliers who was beheaded in the Place de l'Hôtel de Ville in 1676, her body burned and her ashes scattered to the winds for poisoning her family?

So many deaths, so many stories.

Marie Antoinette lived here, Victor Hugo lived there, Mozart visited this courtyard, Stravinsky worked in that studio, Gertrude Stein befriended artists near the Luxembourg Gardens, people who in their youth lived life to the fullest in Paris, rejoicing in the vitality of young dreams and aspirations, lifting their faces to the bright beacon of the Sacre Coeur or the Eiffel Tower; and who were all gone now, remembered by plaques on apartment buildings or markers on street corners.

Though we saw death during our time in Paris, it never came close to us except for Madame Remy. Instead, you were often aware that your life was the momentary flicker of a candle in a city of a million candles–burning in the present and on into the future; or a leaf tumbling from one side of the Notre Dame courtyard to the other, its journey a tracing of your life in the French city.

Once, while a couple we knew were visiting the Arc de Triomphe, someone committed suicide by leaping off the top. The body struck the cobblestones only a few feet behind our friends as they strolled

225

through the Arc. At the sickening thud, the young woman turned to see a crumpled, bloody form on the stones. The jumper had landed head-first and was unrecognizable as a man or woman. The young woman had fainted and her husband grabbed her as she slumped to the ground.

After hearing their story, I wondered if the jumper had waited for them to pass-gazing down at the two black dots from his or her perch atop the Arc-or had our friends evaded death by a footstep?

On another occasion, a friend came over for dinner on a cold evening in January. An ice storm had swept through northern France, causing a loss of electricity in many small towns, accidents on the *Périphérique,* and a delay of train schedules.

As our friend took off his winter coat and ran a hand through his cold hair, he looked at me.

"I just passed a dead man lying in the gutter," he said.

"Where?" I asked.

"On the Boulevard du Temple."

"Maybe he was drunk."

"No," my friend said. "This guy was stone dead. No question."

Numerous *clochards* inhabited that area. I guessed the cold had finally gotten to one of them.

"What did you do?" I asked.

My friend shrugged. "I stepped over him."

***

Our departure from Paris came in a different way.

It was mid-December and Claudia and I were free one evening, with no social engagements to hinder our activities. She wanted to see the Christmas lights, so I suggested we take the Métro to the Avenue Champs-Élysées. The long stretch of twinkling lights from the Arc de Triomphe down to the Jardin des Tuileries was festive and beautiful.

As we strolled along the avenue, I could tell she had something on her mind. Claudia was in her late twenties. We had led an adventurous life in West Africa, Switzerland, and now Paris, and she was ready to settle down and start a family. I, of course, was miles away from ever thinking about this. I still had a list of places I wanted to see and things I wanted to do.

"We could try," she urged, as we reached the Place de la Concorde.

"If you get pregnant, we'll have to leave Paris," I said.

Claudia laughed. "Don't worry. It takes at least a year once you start trying."

"A year?" I asked doubtfully.

"At least," she stressed.

That was in December.

In February I came home one evening and my wife was beaming.

"I'm pregnant!" she gushed.

"What?"

"I'm pregnant!"

I gazed at her. "What happened to my year?"

"You can't plan these things."

"I thought we were?"

She smiled. "Life happens."

I wasn't ready to leave Paris. I *loved* living in Paris. Perhaps in another five years …

We went out for dinner to celebrate and then walked around the Latin Quarter.

I waited.

I knew it was coming.

I didn't want to hear it.

"We can't stay here," she said. "I love Paris too, but we don't have any health insurance."

My head sank. I felt as if someone had kicked me in the stomach.

"I know," I said. "I'll start looking for jobs in the states."

That was on a Tuesday evening.

On Friday, I got a phone call from a friend in San Francisco.

"We have a position for a public relations specialist," he announced. "I think you'd be perfect for the job. Are you interested?"

I held the phone to my ear and gazed at Claudia.

"Who is it?" she asked.

I told her and then about the job offer. It paid well and had excellent benefits.

"That's wonderful!" she exclaimed.

My eyes narrowed. "Did you know about this?"

Claudia was friends with this man's wife.

"No," she replied.

Her sparkling brown eyes were wide. I believed her.

"We'll need you here in April," my friend said.

We talked for a few more minutes and then hung up.

"This is a God thing," Claudia said.

"It's something," I muttered.

I spent the next few months walking around Paris in despair. It wasn't my most manly hour, but I was grieving the loss of a life–and a life direction–I loved.

My last day of teaching turned out to be a blustery, sunny, cloudy, sometimes rainy day. After my class, I walked up to the Luxembourg Gardens. The clouds had parted for a while and many people were sunning themselves in chairs on the gravel paths and around the fountain.

I sat on a chair and thought how I would miss the small things about life in Paris: the scent of the cleaner they used in apartments and cafes, the churn of buses on the streets, the smooth cobblestones in the Latin Quarter, the smell of fresh-baked baguettes in the boulangeries, wandering on Sunday afternoons across the Pont St.-Michel to Notre Dame Cathedral, the view of Paris from the Sacre Coeur, sitting for hours with friends at cafés, walking the horse-chestnut lined streets, the eternal fascination and tedium of the Métro, and always the possibility of excitement and adventure at the train stations–especially the Gare du Nord.

When I got home, Claudia was waiting for me.

"I'm not leaving," she announced.

"What?" I asked.

"Marie is driving to the south of France for two weeks. She asked me to go with her."

"Are you serious? I was about to buy our plane tickets. You're not going with me to San Francisco?"

"It's only two weeks," she said. "I don't need to be there. You'll be starting your job."

"And finding a place to live?"

"Yes."

I gazed around our apartment.

"You'll have to move out of here."

"Bobby said I could stay at his place. He's going back to Toronto for a few weeks."

"So, you've got it all worked out," I said, feeling I'd been played. I didn't want to leave Paris. Now that I was buying my plane ticket, *she* decided not to leave. I felt slightly bitter.

I flew out of Charles de Gaulle Airport the next weekend. The afternoon before my flight, I walked around the Left Bank and tried to take photographs of everything I would miss, but it wasn't the same. Photos couldn't capture the feelings I had about Paris.

Claudia and Marie had a pleasant vacation in Provence. On her return to Paris, she settled into Bobby's apartment. Two days later, she returned from the market to find his door open. This was unusual. Perhaps he had flown home early from Toronto.

"Bobby!" she called, peeking through the door.

There was no response, but she could hear someone rummaging in the back bedroom.

"Bobby!"

The noise stopped.

Tentatively, Claudia took a few steps into the apartment and listened. There was silence for several seconds and then a man's head slowly appeared around the bedroom door frame.

It wasn't Bobby.

This man had dark hair, an olive-skinned complexion, and black beady eyes.

He and Claudia gazed at each other for a moment, and then he exploded out of the doorway and rushed toward her.

Claudia had an interesting way of dealing with fear and danger. She froze. Once we were in an old movie theater in Daloa when a ceiling fan caught fire. Flames shot up the fan to the ceiling. Within seconds, people were stampeding up the crowded aisles. One of our friends ran across the top of the seats to get out. In the confusion, a woman dropped her baby. Another of our friends saved the child from being trampled and carried it outside.

During all this time, Claudia was frozen solid. I'd never seen this reaction by anyone before.

Now a thief was charging her in Bobby's apartment and again she didn't move.

Grabbing her by the shoulders, the thief slammed her fiercely into the wall. Then he ran out the door and down the stairs. He was carrying a bag.

Three months pregnant, Claudia was badly shaken, but not seriously injured.

This was our last memory of Paris—a beautiful French life experience, followed by a robbery and mugging. The thief stole everything of value in Bobby's apartment, including Claudia's jewelry.

***

When you're young and excited about life, the future holds a promise of adventure and romance and success. It's intriguing to look back on those Paris days now and think how naïve we all were; not realizing the excitement and adventure we so eagerly desired was happening around us; before our eyes, and with an intensity we would not appreciate until a few years later-and never again be able to duplicate.

Yet, as Helen Keller stated: What we have once enjoyed we can never lose. All that we love deeply becomes a part of us.

Paris certainly became a part of me. I have only to close my eyes and I can see the pearl-colored sky, crowded boulevards, sidewalk cafes, old stone bridges, and apartment buildings damp in the rain. I can feel the soft gravel of the Luxembourg Gardens underfoot, sense the wind against my face as I cross the Pont Neuf, or see my friends gathered at the Café La Palette. I'm also reminded that while rounding a corner on the rue de Malte, you can smack head-long into an elephant.

This is what makes life in the French city exciting.

Postscript
Yellow Blossoms in the Typewriter Keys

After our first year in Paris, we spent the summer teaching at a school in Switzerland. The school was nestled in Montagnola in the scenic foothills of the Swiss/Italian Alps, just down the hill from the village where Herman Hesse had lived.

One afternoon I was browsing through the school library when I picked up a novel by the British writer Graham Greene. It was *The Quiet American*. The opening scene describes a beautiful Vietnamese girl, the scent of opium smoking, and yellow blossoms falling among the keys of the journalist's typewriter. And I thought, Wow!

I read the novel that summer and purchased a copy for myself as soon as we got back to Paris. I can still remember walking out of W.H. Smiths to the covered walkway along the Rue de Rivoli with the book in my hand. If Beethoven's music had given me a sense of texture and intensity, and Faulkner had introduced me to a flowing, deep, eternal rhythm in prose, then the writing of Greene had given me a tone, a world-experience, a cynical way of viewing life that suited my temperament.

That year I read everything I could get my hands on by Greene—my favorites being *The Quiet American, The Heart of the Matter, The Third Man,* and *Ways of Escape.*

In December, I heard he was living in Antibes, in the south of France. A journalist friend gave me his address and I sent Greene a brief note thanking him for his work. He responded quickly and we began a correspondence.

At one point—out of youth and naiveté, or temerity, you might say—I dared to tell him that although I loved *The Quiet American,* (it truly is one of my favorite novels) the motivations of the protagonist Thomas Fowler troubled me.

I wrote:

I admire his experienced apathy and emotional jadedness, and yet – as a narrator-he seems unreliable. The conclusion of the novel seems to negate the opening chapter where Fowler explains he is waiting for Pyle, when in reality, he assumes Pyle is dead. Inspector Vigot wasn't so far wrong then in his assessment of Fowler's implication in the death.

To me, it appears Fowler is as directly responsible for Pyle's death as if he had pressed the young American's head into the river mud himself. This creates a problem. For if one scene in a book is unreliable, isn't it possible other incidents are also misleading? I'm referring to Fowler's motive in setting up Pyle. Wasn't this, after all, merely a means for the older man to rid himself of the young American and get back Phuong? And not really concerning his feelings about becoming engagé?

After Pyle's death, Fowler's life takes a dramatic upswing. He is allowed to remain in Vietnam as a correspondent, receives a divorce telegram from his wife, and reunites with his Vietnamese mistress. With his closing demand for forgiveness, isn't he indirectly stating that murder pays?

Mr. Greene was very kind in his response. I add his letter here for readers who appreciate his work, and for those who enjoy *The Quiet American*. Perhaps it will give some insights to the author's thoughts on the novel, and a better understanding of his writing style.

Dear Mr. Corey,

Thank you for your letter and the nice things you write about my work. I think you have a little misread the opening chapter of The Quiet American. Fowler records the conversation with Vigot which of course is a very carefully phrased one to guard himself. But until Vigot's questions show him that Pyle is dead he is not certain of it. Although he has signaled to the Vietnim an indication of Pyle's movements that night he hopes against hope that Pyle will have escaped. So, in a sense he is still waiting for Pyle, hoping that he may after all turn up. You have to remember that the point of view throughout is Fowler's and Fowler's motives are mixed. Jealousy of Pyle over Phuong is one motive and his horror at the bomb outside the Continental in which Pyle is obviously concerned is another motive. The telegram from his wife a cruel irony at the end. I wouldn't describe his remark at the end as being a demand for forgiveness. It's only a regret that he has no religious faith and therefore he can't ask for forgiveness.

Yours sincerely,
Graham Green

CPSIA information can be obtained
at www.ICGtesting.com
Printed in the USA
BVHW041752080223
658145BV00005B/99